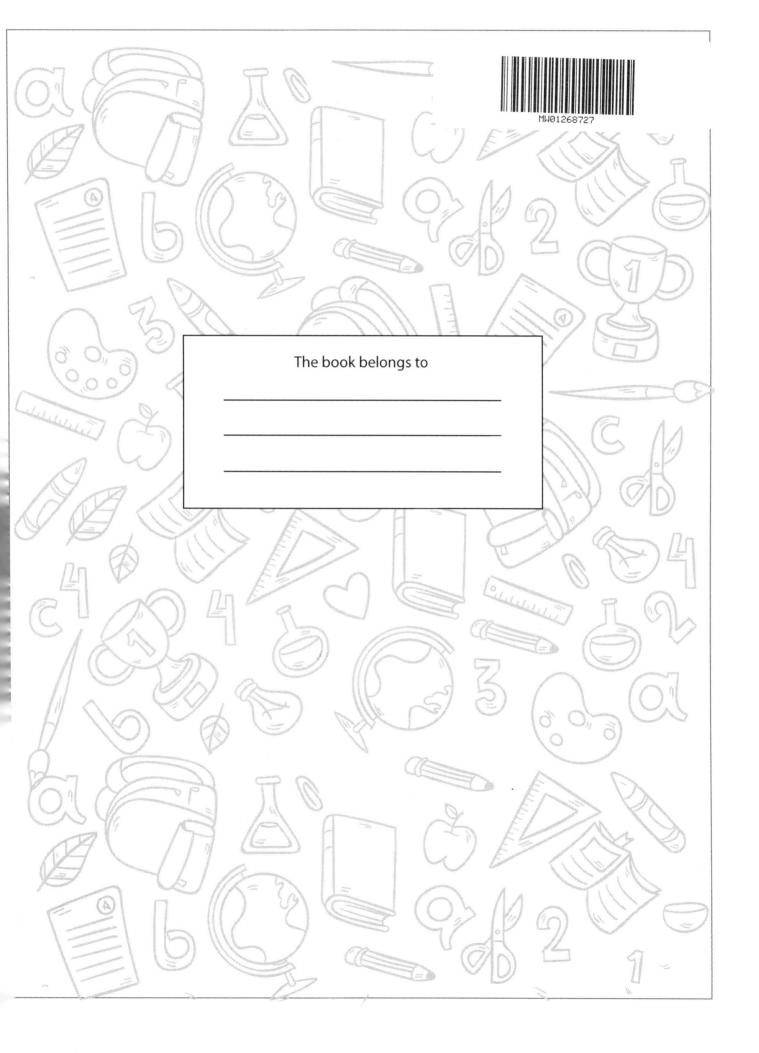

The book belongs to

_____

_____

_____

About the book

Kids assessment levels in this book has been mainly designed for evaluating all types of development of Preschool children. The cognitive and affective developments of kids , are formed in the early stages . So to enhance these developments in children, they need a rich ,stimulating learning environment that has to be well crafted and well planned. Nowadays in Preschools, they provide a very friendly learning environment , which kids craving for. So this book is a powerful tool for all the teachers who are handling kids in kindergarten level. There are 3 assessments for each child in this book. So teachers can utilize this book for one year to improve the child in a 3 term basis.

For more creative books and Journals, please check author P Parithipriyan in Amazon.com

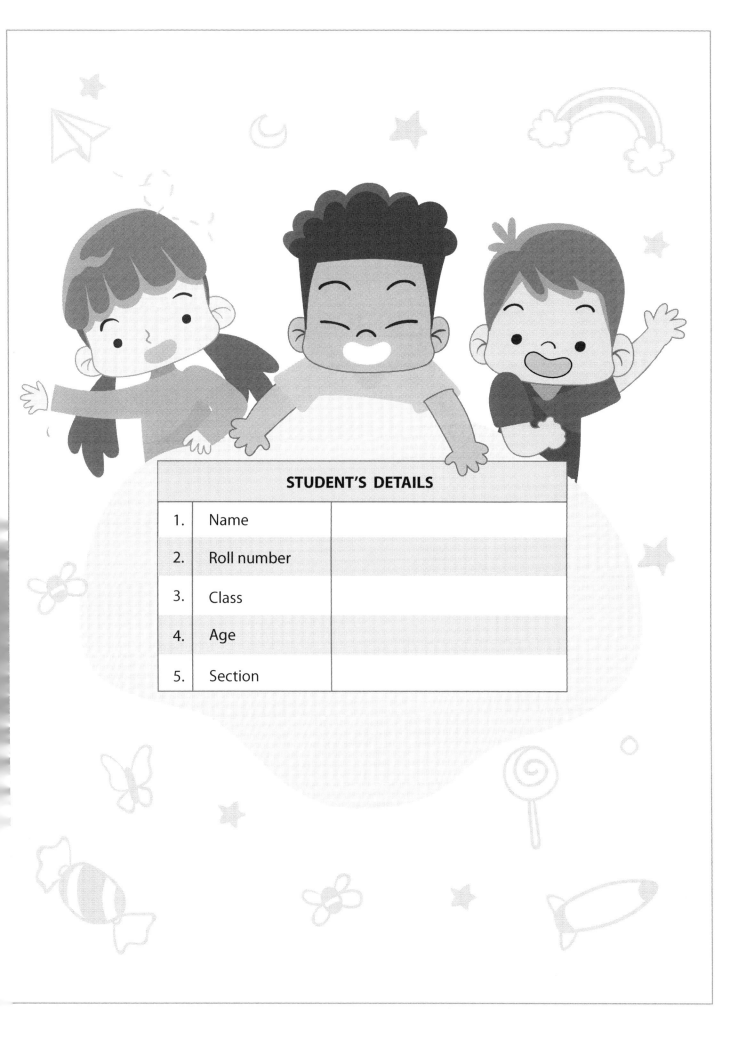

STUDENT'S DETAILS

1.	Name	
2.	Roll number	
3.	Class	
4.	Age	
5.	Section	

NAME : _____

PHYSICAL DEVELOPMENT

GROSS MOTOR SKILLS		A	B	C
1.	Walks with proper balance			
2.	Hops on one foot			
3.	Jumps			
4.	Catches and throws a ball			
5.	Steps over circles			
6.	Marches with swinging arms			
7.	Skips			
8.	Balances on one foot			

FINE MOTOR SKILLS		A	B	C
1.	Tears newspaper into strips			
2.	Crushes paper into ball			
3.	Picks up tiny objects			
4.	Buttons shirts			
5.	Draws in wet sand			
6.	Opens and closes the door			
7.	Builds tower with building blocks			
8.	Rolls clay into balls			

A	PERFECT DEMONSTRATION OF SKILL	B	PROGRESSING TOWARDS SKILL	C	NEEDS IMPROVEMENT

SKILLS AND COMPETENCIES

LISTENING AND SPEAKING SKILLS	A	B	C
1. Recognises sounds and rhymes			
2. Follows instructions			
3. Asks and answers questions			
4. Listen to stories			
5. Speaks clearly			
6. Repeats rhymes with actions			
7. Tells stories using pictures			
8. Describes experiences			

WRITING AND CREATIVE SKILLS	A	B	C
1. Traces patterns, letters and objects			
2. Fills colours			
3. Writes letters and words			
4. Writes missing letters			
5. Draws and matches objects			
6. Makes models by using clay & paper			
7. Predicts what comes next			
8. Solving easy puzzles & problems			

A	PERFECT DEMONSTRATION OF SKILL	B	PROGRESSING TOWARDS SKILL	C	NEEDS IMPROVEMENT

SKILLS AND COMPETENCIES

	LIFE SKILLS	A	B	C
1.	Hand and eye coordination			
2.	Eats on his or her own			
3.	Ask for help if needed			
4.	Sharing with others			
5.	Expresses likes and dislikes			
6.	Shows gratitude and thanks			
7.	Shows respect and kindness to elders			
8.	Cares for others, animals and plants			

	VISUAL & DISCRIMINATION SKILLS	A	B	C
1.	Identifies objects, pictures & persons			
2.	Finds the object or person in the pic			
3.	Sorts objects of same size & colour			
4.	Matches objects			
5.	Finds the odd one out			
6.	Understands the position & direction			
7.	Identifies the shapes, colours & size			
8.	Understand the distance			

Teacher's Signature	

A	PERFECT DEMONSTRATION OF SKILL	**B**	PROGRESSING TOWARDS SKILL	**C**	NEEDS IMPROVEMENT

ASSESSMENT - 2

NAME : _____

PHYSICAL DEVELOPMENT

	GROSS MOTOR SKILLS	A	B	C
1.	Walks with proper balance			
2.	Hops on one foot			
3.	Jumps			
4.	Catches and throws a ball			
5.	Steps over circles			
6.	Marches with swinging arms			
7.	Skips			
8.	Balances on one foot			

	FINE MOTOR SKILLS	A	B	C
1.	Tears newspaper into strips			
2.	Crushes paper into ball			
3.	Picks up tiny objects			
4.	Buttons shirts			
5.	Draws in wet sand			
6.	Opens and closes the door			
7.	Builds tower with building blocks			
8.	Rolls clay into balls			

A	PERFECT DEMONSTRATION OF SKILL	B	PROGRESSING TOWARDS SKILL	C	NEEDS IMPROVEMENT

SKILLS AND COMPETENCIES

LISTENING AND SPEAKING SKILLS		A	B	C
1.	Recognises sounds and rhymes			
2.	Follows instructions			
3.	Asks and answers questions			
4.	Listen to stories			
5.	Speaks clearly			
6.	Repeats rhymes with actions			
7.	Tells stories using pictures			
8.	Describes experiences			

WRITING AND CREATIVE SKILLS		A	B	C
1.	Traces patterns, letters and objects			
2.	Fills colours			
3.	Writes letters and words			
4.	Writes missing letters			
5.	Draws and matches objects			
6.	Makes models by using clay & paper			
7.	Predicts what comes next			
8.	Solving easy puzzles & problems			

A	PERFECT DEMONSTRATION OF SKILL	B	PROGRESSING TOWARDS SKILL	C	NEEDS IMPROVEMENT

SKILLS AND COMPETENCIES

LIFE SKILLS		A	B	C
1.	Hand and eye coordination			
2.	Eats on his or her own			
3.	Ask for help if needed			
4.	Sharing with others			
5.	Expresses likes and dislikes			
6.	Shows gratitude and thanks			
7.	Shows respect and kindness to elders			
8.	Cares for others, animals and plants			

VISUAL & DISCRIMINATION SKILLS		A	B	C
1.	Identifies objects, pictures & persons			
2.	Finds the object or person in the pic			
3.	Sorts objects of same size & colour			
4.	Matches objects			
5.	Finds the odd one out			
6.	Understands the position & direction			
7.	Identifies the shapes, colours & size			
8.	Understand the distance			

Teacher's Signature	

A	PERFECT DEMONSTRATION OF SKILL	**B**	PROGRESSING TOWARDS SKILL	**C**	NEEDS IMPROVEMENT

PHYSICAL DEVELOPMENT

GROSS MOTOR SKILLS		A	B	C
1.	Walks with proper balance			
2.	Hops on one foot			
3.	Jumps			
4.	Catches and throws a ball			
5.	Steps over circles			
6.	Marches with swinging arms			
7.	Skips			
8.	Balances on one foot			

FINE MOTOR SKILLS		A	B	C
1.	Tears newspaper into strips			
2.	Crushes paper into ball			
3.	Picks up tiny objects			
4.	Buttons shirts			
5.	Draws in wet sand			
6.	Opens and closes the door			
7.	Builds tower with building blocks			
8.	Rolls clay into balls			

| **A** | PERFECT DEMONSTRATION OF SKILL | **B** | PROGRESSING TOWARDS SKILL | **C** | NEEDS IMPROVEMENT |

NAME : _____

SKILLS AND COMPETENCIES

LISTENING AND SPEAKING SKILLS	A	B	C
1. Recognises sounds and rhymes			
2. Follows instructions			
3. Asks and answers questions			
4. Listen to stories			
5. Speaks clearly			
6. Repeats rhymes with actions			
7. Tells stories using pictures			
8. Describes experiences			

WRITING AND CREATIVE SKILLS	A	B	C
1. Traces patterns, letters and objects			
2. Fills colours			
3. Writes letters and words			
4. Writes missing letters			
5. Draws and matches objects			
6. Makes models by using clay & paper			
7. Predicts what comes next			
8. Solving easy puzzles & problems			

A	PERFECT DEMONSTRATION OF SKILL	B	PROGRESSING TOWARDS SKILL	C	NEEDS IMPROVEMENT

NAME : _____

SKILLS AND COMPETENCIES

	LIFE SKILLS	A	B	C
1.	Hand and eye coordination			
2.	Eats on his or her own			
3.	Ask for help if needed			
4.	Sharing with others			
5.	Expresses likes and dislikes			
6.	Shows gratitude and thanks			
7.	Shows respect and kindness to elders			
8.	Cares for others, animals and plants			

	VISUAL & DISCRIMINATION SKILLS	A	B	C
1.	Identifies objects, pictures & persons			
2.	Finds the object or person in the pic			
3.	Sorts objects of same size & colour			
4.	Matches objects			
5.	Finds the odd one out			
6.	Understands the position & direction			
7.	Identifies the shapes, colours & size			
8.	Understand the distance			

Teacher's Signature	

A	PERFECT DEMONSTRATION OF SKILL	**B**	PROGRESSING TOWARDS SKILL	**C**	NEEDS IMPROVEMENT

STUDENT'S DETAILS

1.	Name	
2.	Roll number	
3.	Class	
4.	Age	
5.	Section	

PHYSICAL DEVELOPMENT

GROSS MOTOR SKILLS		A	B	C
1.	Walks with proper balance			
2.	Hops on one foot			
3.	Jumps			
4.	Catches and throws a ball			
5.	Steps over circles			
6.	Marches with swinging arms			
7.	Skips			
8.	Balances on one foot			

FINE MOTOR SKILLS		A	B	C
1.	Tears newspaper into strips			
2.	Crushes paper into ball			
3.	Picks up tiny objects			
4.	Buttons shirts			
5.	Draws in wet sand			
6.	Opens and closes the door			
7.	Builds tower with building blocks			
8.	Rolls clay into balls			

A	PERFECT DEMONSTRATION OF SKILL	B	PROGRESSING TOWARDS SKILL	C	NEEDS IMPROVEMENT

SKILLS AND COMPETENCIES

LISTENING AND SPEAKING SKILLS	A	B	C
1. Recognises sounds and rhymes			
2. Follows instructions			
3. Asks and answers questions			
4. Listen to stories			
5. Speaks clearly			
6. Repeats rhymes with actions			
7. Tells stories using pictures			
8. Describes experiences			

WRITING AND CREATIVE SKILLS	A	B	C
1. Traces patterns, letters and objects			
2. Fills colours			
3. Writes letters and words			
4. Writes missing letters			
5. Draws and matches objects			
6. Makes models by using clay & paper			
7. Predicts what comes next			
8. Solving easy puzzles & problems			

A	PERFECT DEMONSTRATION OF SKILL	B	PROGRESSING TOWARDS SKILL	C	NEEDS IMPROVEMENT

ASSESSMENT - 1

NAME : _____

SKILLS AND COMPETENCIES

	LIFE SKILLS	A	B	C
1.	Hand and eye coordination			
2.	Eats on his or her own			
3.	Ask for help if needed			
4.	Sharing with others			
5.	Expresses likes and dislikes			
6.	Shows gratitude and thanks			
7.	Shows respect and kindness to elders			
8.	Cares for others, animals and plants			

	VISUAL & DISCRIMINATION SKILLS	A	B	C
1.	Identifies objects, pictures & persons			
2.	Finds the object or person in the pic			
3.	Sorts objects of same size & colour			
4.	Matches objects			
5.	Finds the odd one out			
6.	Understands the position & direction			
7.	Identifies the shapes, colours & size			
8.	Understand the distance			

Teacher's Signature	

A	PERFECT DEMONSTRATION OF SKILL	B	PROGRESSING TOWARDS SKILL	C	NEEDS IMPROVEMENT

PHYSICAL DEVELOPMENT

GROSS MOTOR SKILLS		A	B	C
1.	Walks with proper balance			
2.	Hops on one foot			
3.	Jumps			
4.	Catches and throws a ball			
5.	Steps over circles			
6.	Marches with swinging arms			
7.	Skips			
8.	Balances on one foot			

FINE MOTOR SKILLS		A	B	C
1.	Tears newspaper into strips			
2.	Crushes paper into ball			
3.	Picks up tiny objects			
4.	Buttons shirts			
5.	Draws in wet sand			
6.	Opens and closes the door			
7.	Builds tower with building blocks			
8.	Rolls clay into balls			

A	PERFECT DEMONSTRATION OF SKILL	B	PROGRESSING TOWARDS SKILL	C	NEEDS IMPROVEMENT

SKILLS AND COMPETENCIES

LISTENING AND SPEAKING SKILLS	A	B	C
1. Recognises sounds and rhymes			
2. Follows instructions			
3. Asks and answers questions			
4. Listen to stories			
5. Speaks clearly			
6. Repeats rhymes with actions			
7. Tells stories using pictures			
8. Describes experiences			

WRITING AND CREATIVE SKILLS	A	B	C
1. Traces patterns, letters and objects			
2. Fills colours			
3. Writes letters and words			
4. Writes missing letters			
5. Draws and matches objects			
6. Makes models by using clay & paper			
7. Predicts what comes next			
8. Solving easy puzzles & problems			

A PERFECT DEMONSTRATION OF SKILL	**B** PROGRESSING TOWARDS SKILL	**C** NEEDS IMPROVEMENT

ASSESSMENT - 2

NAME : _____

SKILLS AND COMPETENCIES

	LIFE SKILLS	A	B	C
1.	Hand and eye coordination			
2.	Eats on his or her own			
3.	Ask for help if needed			
4.	Sharing with others			
5.	Expresses likes and dislikes			
6.	Shows gratitude and thanks			
7.	Shows respect and kindness to elders			
8.	Cares for others, animals and plants			

	VISUAL & DISCRIMINATION SKILLS	A	B	C
1.	Identifies objects, pictures & persons			
2.	Finds the object or person in the pic			
3.	Sorts objects of same size & colour			
4.	Matches objects			
5.	Finds the odd one out			
6.	Understands the position & direction			
7.	Identifies the shapes, colours & size			
8.	Understand the distance			

Teacher's Signature	

A PERFECT DEMONSTRATION OF SKILL **B** PROGRESSING TOWARDS SKILL **C** NEEDS IMPROVEMENT

PHYSICAL DEVELOPMENT

GROSS MOTOR SKILLS		A	B	C
1.	Walks with proper balance			
2.	Hops on one foot			
3.	Jumps			
4.	Catches and throws a ball			
5.	Steps over circles			
6.	Marches with swinging arms			
7.	Skips			
8.	Balances on one foot			

FINE MOTOR SKILLS		A	B	C
1.	Tears newspaper into strips			
2.	Crushes paper into ball			
3.	Picks up tiny objects			
4.	Buttons shirts			
5.	Draws in wet sand			
6.	Opens and closes the door			
7.	Builds tower with building blocks			
8.	Rolls clay into balls			

| **A** | PERFECT DEMONSTRATION OF SKILL | **B** | PROGRESSING TOWARDS SKILL | **C** | NEEDS IMPROVEMENT |

SKILLS AND COMPETENCIES

LISTENING AND SPEAKING SKILLS	A	B	C
1. Recognises sounds and rhymes			
2. Follows instructions			
3. Asks and answers questions			
4. Listen to stories			
5. Speaks clearly			
6. Repeats rhymes with actions			
7. Tells stories using pictures			
8. Describes experiences			

WRITING AND CREATIVE SKILLS	A	B	C
1. Traces patterns, letters and objects			
2. Fills colours			
3. Writes letters and words			
4. Writes missing letters			
5. Draws and matches objects			
6. Makes models by using clay & paper			
7. Predicts what comes next			
8. Solving easy puzzles & problems			

A	PERFECT DEMONSTRATION OF SKILL	B	PROGRESSING TOWARDS SKILL	C	NEEDS IMPROVEMENT

SKILLS AND COMPETENCIES

	LIFE SKILLS	A	B	C
1.	Hand and eye coordination			
2.	Eats on his or her own			
3.	Ask for help if needed			
4.	Sharing with others			
5.	Expresses likes and dislikes			
6.	Shows gratitude and thanks			
7.	Shows respect and kindness to elders			
8.	Cares for others, animals and plants			

	VISUAL & DISCRIMINATION SKILLS	A	B	C
1.	Identifies objects, pictures & persons			
2.	Finds the object or person in the pic			
3.	Sorts objects of same size & colour			
4.	Matches objects			
5.	Finds the odd one out			
6.	Understands the position & direction			
7.	Identifies the shapes, colours & size			
8.	Understand the distance			

Teacher's Signature	

A	PERFECT DEMONSTRATION OF SKILL	**B**	PROGRESSING TOWARDS SKILL	**C**	NEEDS IMPROVEMENT

STUDENT'S DETAILS

1.	Name	
2.	Roll number	
3.	Class	
4.	Age	
5.	Section	

PHYSICAL DEVELOPMENT

GROSS MOTOR SKILLS		A	B	C
1.	Walks with proper balance			
2.	Hops on one foot			
3.	Jumps			
4.	Catches and throws a ball			
5.	Steps over circles			
6.	Marches with swinging arms			
7.	Skips			
8.	Balances on one foot			

FINE MOTOR SKILLS		A	B	C
1.	Tears newspaper into strips			
2.	Crushes paper into ball			
3.	Picks up tiny objects			
4.	Buttons shirts			
5.	Draws in wet sand			
6.	Opens and closes the door			
7.	Builds tower with building blocks			
8.	Rolls clay into balls			

A	PERFECT DEMONSTRATION OF SKILL	B	PROGRESSING TOWARDS SKILL	C	NEEDS IMPROVEMENT

ASSESSMENT - 1

NAME : _____

SKILLS AND COMPETENCIES

LISTENING AND SPEAKING SKILLS		A	B	C
1.	Recognises sounds and rhymes			
2.	Follows instructions			
3.	Asks and answers questions			
4.	Listen to stories			
5.	Speaks clearly			
6.	Repeats rhymes with actions			
7.	Tells stories using pictures			
8.	Describes experiences			

WRITING AND CREATIVE SKILLS		A	B	C
1.	Traces patterns, letters and objects			
2.	Fills colours			
3.	Writes letters and words			
4.	Writes missing letters			
5.	Draws and matches objects			
6.	Makes models by using clay & paper			
7.	Predicts what comes next			
8.	Solving easy puzzles & problems			

A PERFECT DEMONSTRATION OF SKILL	**B** PROGRESSING TOWARDS SKILL	**C** NEEDS IMPROVEMENT

ASSESSMENT - 1

NAME : _____

SKILLS AND COMPETENCIES

LIFE SKILLS		A	B	C
1.	Hand and eye coordination			
2.	Eats on his or her own			
3.	Ask for help if needed			
4.	Sharing with others			
5.	Expresses likes and dislikes			
6.	Shows gratitude and thanks			
7.	Shows respect and kindness to elders			
8.	Cares for others, animals and plants			

VISUAL & DISCRIMINATION SKILLS		A	B	C
1.	Identifies objects, pictures & persons			
2.	Finds the object or person in the pic			
3.	Sorts objects of same size & colour			
4.	Matches objects			
5.	Finds the odd one out			
6.	Understands the position & direction			
7.	Identifies the shapes, colours & size			
8.	Understand the distance			

Teacher's Signature	

A	PERFECT DEMONSTRATION OF SKILL	**B**	PROGRESSING TOWARDS SKILL	**C**	NEEDS IMPROVEMENT

PHYSICAL DEVELOPMENT

GROSS MOTOR SKILLS	A	B	C
1. Walks with proper balance			
2. Hops on one foot			
3. Jumps			
4. Catches and throws a ball			
5. Steps over circles			
6. Marches with swinging arms			
7. Skips			
8. Balances on one foot			

FINE MOTOR SKILLS	A	B	C
1. Tears newspaper into strips			
2. Crushes paper into ball			
3. Picks up tiny objects			
4. Buttons shirts			
5. Draws in wet sand			
6. Opens and closes the door			
7. Builds tower with building blocks			
8. Rolls clay into balls			

A	PERFECT DEMONSTRATION OF SKILL	B	PROGRESSING TOWARDS SKILL	C	NEEDS IMPROVEMENT

SKILLS AND COMPETENCIES

LISTENING AND SPEAKING SKILLS		A	B	C
1.	Recognises sounds and rhymes			
2.	Follows instructions			
3.	Asks and answers questions			
4.	Listen to stories			
5.	Speaks clearly			
6.	Repeats rhymes with actions			
7.	Tells stories using pictures			
8.	Describes experiences			

WRITING AND CREATIVE SKILLS		A	B	C
1.	Traces patterns, letters and objects			
2.	Fills colours			
3.	Writes letters and words			
4.	Writes missing letters			
5.	Draws and matches objects			
6.	Makes models by using clay & paper			
7.	Predicts what comes next			
8.	Solving easy puzzles & problems			

A	PERFECT DEMONSTRATION OF SKILL	B	PROGRESSING TOWARDS SKILL	C	NEEDS IMPROVEMENT

SKILLS AND COMPETENCIES

	LIFE SKILLS	A	B	C
1.	Hand and eye coordination			
2.	Eats on his or her own			
3.	Ask for help if needed			
4.	Sharing with others			
5.	Expresses likes and dislikes			
6.	Shows gratitude and thanks			
7.	Shows respect and kindness to elders			
8.	Cares for others, animals and plants			

	VISUAL & DISCRIMINATION SKILLS	A	B	C
1.	Identifies objects, pictures & persons			
2.	Finds the object or person in the pic			
3.	Sorts objects of same size & colour			
4.	Matches objects			
5.	Finds the odd one out			
6.	Understands the position & direction			
7.	Identifies the shapes, colours & size			
8.	Understand the distance			

Teacher's Signature	

A	PERFECT DEMONSTRATION OF SKILL	**B**	PROGRESSING TOWARDS SKILL	**C**	NEEDS IMPROVEMENT

PHYSICAL DEVELOPMENT

GROSS MOTOR SKILLS		A	B	C
1.	Walks with proper balance			
2.	Hops on one foot			
3.	Jumps			
4.	Catches and throws a ball			
5.	Steps over circles			
6.	Marches with swinging arms			
7.	Skips			
8.	Balances on one foot			

FINE MOTOR SKILLS		A	B	C
1.	Tears newspaper into strips			
2.	Crushes paper into ball			
3.	Picks up tiny objects			
4.	Buttons shirts			
5.	Draws in wet sand			
6.	Opens and closes the door			
7.	Builds tower with building blocks			
8.	Rolls clay into balls			

A	PERFECT DEMONSTRATION OF SKILL	B	PROGRESSING TOWARDS SKILL	C	NEEDS IMPROVEMENT

SKILLS AND COMPETENCIES

LISTENING AND SPEAKING SKILLS	A	B	C
1. Recognises sounds and rhymes			
2. Follows instructions			
3. Asks and answers questions			
4. Listen to stories			
5. Speaks clearly			
6. Repeats rhymes with actions			
7. Tells stories using pictures			
8. Describes experiences			

WRITING AND CREATIVE SKILLS	A	B	C
1. Traces patterns, letters and objects			
2. Fills colours			
3. Writes letters and words			
4. Writes missing letters			
5. Draws and matches objects			
6. Makes models by using clay & paper			
7. Predicts what comes next			
8. Solving easy puzzles & problems			

A	PERFECT DEMONSTRATION OF SKILL	B	PROGRESSING TOWARDS SKILL	C	NEEDS IMPROVEMENT

ASSESSMENT - 3   NAME : _____

SKILLS AND COMPETENCIES

LIFE SKILLS		A	B	C
1.	Hand and eye coordination			
2.	Eats on his or her own			
3.	Ask for help if needed			
4.	Sharing with others			
5.	Expresses likes and dislikes			
6.	Shows gratitude and thanks			
7.	Shows respect and kindness to elders			
8.	Cares for others, animals and plants			

VISUAL & DISCRIMINATION SKILLS		A	B	C
1.	Identifies objects, pictures & persons			
2.	Finds the object or person in the pic			
3.	Sorts objects of same size & colour			
4.	Matches objects			
5.	Finds the odd one out			
6.	Understands the position & direction			
7.	Identifies the shapes, colours & size			
8.	Understand the distance			

Teacher's Signature	

A PERFECT DEMONSTRATION OF SKILL	**B** PROGRESSING TOWARDS SKILL	**C** NEEDS IMPROVEMENT

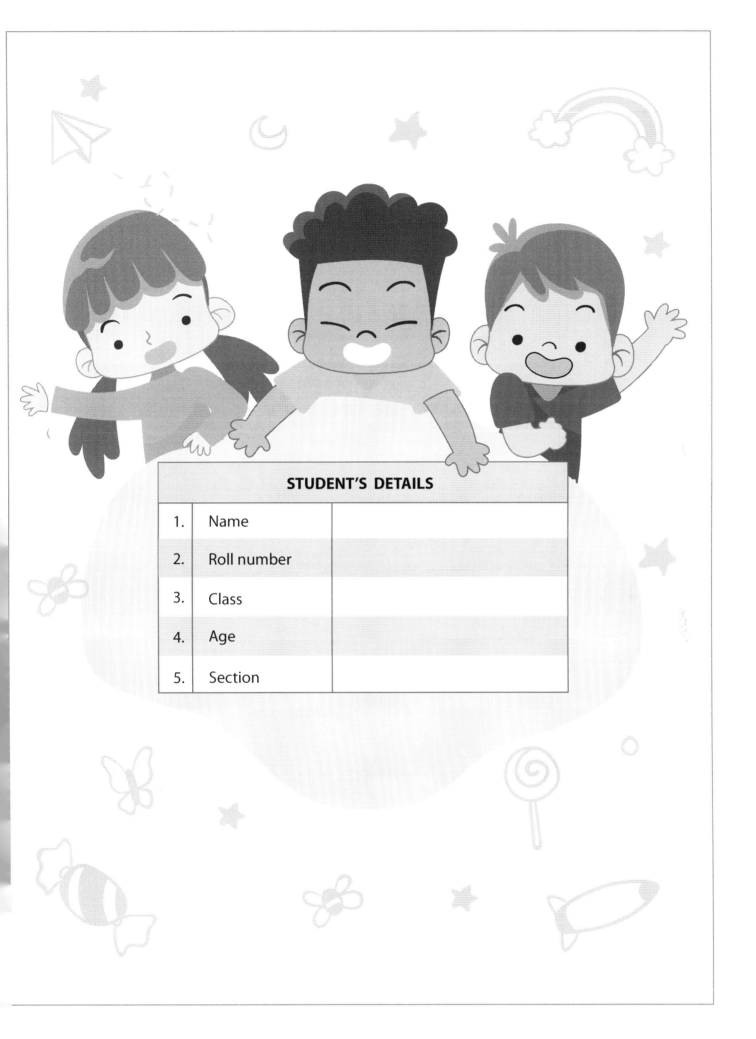

STUDENT'S DETAILS

1.	Name	
2.	Roll number	
3.	Class	
4.	Age	
5.	Section	

PHYSICAL DEVELOPMENT

GROSS MOTOR SKILLS		A	B	C
1.	Walks with proper balance			
2.	Hops on one foot			
3.	Jumps			
4.	Catches and throws a ball			
5.	Steps over circles			
6.	Marches with swinging arms			
7.	Skips			
8.	Balances on one foot			

FINE MOTOR SKILLS		A	B	C
1.	Tears newspaper into strips			
2.	Crushes paper into ball			
3.	Picks up tiny objects			
4.	Buttons shirts			
5.	Draws in wet sand			
6.	Opens and closes the door			
7.	Builds tower with building blocks			
8.	Rolls clay into balls			

A	PERFECT DEMONSTRATION OF SKILL	B	PROGRESSING TOWARDS SKILL	C	NEEDS IMPROVEMENT

ASSESSMENT - 1

NAME : _____

SKILLS AND COMPETENCIES

LISTENING AND SPEAKING SKILLS		A	B	C
1.	Recognises sounds and rhymes			
2.	Follows instructions			
3.	Asks and answers questions			
4.	Listen to stories			
5.	Speaks clearly			
6.	Repeats rhymes with actions			
7.	Tells stories using pictures			
8.	Describes experiences			

WRITING AND CREATIVE SKILLS		A	B	C
1.	Traces patterns, letters and objects			
2.	Fills colours			
3.	Writes letters and words			
4.	Writes missing letters			
5.	Draws and matches objects			
6.	Makes models by using clay & paper			
7.	Predicts what comes next			
8.	Solving easy puzzles & problems			

A PERFECT DEMONSTRATION OF SKILL	**B** PROGRESSING TOWARDS SKILL	**C** NEEDS IMPROVEMENT

ASSESSMENT - 1

NAME : _____

SKILLS AND COMPETENCIES

LIFE SKILLS		A	B	C
1.	Hand and eye coordination			
2.	Eats on his or her own			
3.	Ask for help if needed			
4.	Sharing with others			
5.	Expresses likes and dislikes			
6.	Shows gratitude and thanks			
7.	Shows respect and kindness to elders			
8.	Cares for others, animals and plants			

VISUAL & DISCRIMINATION SKILLS		A	B	C
1.	Identifies objects, pictures & persons			
2.	Finds the object or person in the pic			
3.	Sorts objects of same size & colour			
4.	Matches objects			
5.	Finds the odd one out			
6.	Understands the position & direction			
7.	Identifies the shapes, colours & size			
8.	Understand the distance			

Teacher's Signature	

A	PERFECT DEMONSTRATION OF SKILL	**B**	PROGRESSING TOWARDS SKILL	**C**	NEEDS IMPROVEMENT

NAME : _____

PHYSICAL DEVELOPMENT

GROSS MOTOR SKILLS		A	B	C
1.	Walks with proper balance			
2.	Hops on one foot			
3.	Jumps			
4.	Catches and throws a ball			
5.	Steps over circles			
6.	Marches with swinging arms			
7.	Skips			
8.	Balances on one foot			

FINE MOTOR SKILLS		A	B	C
1.	Tears newspaper into strips			
2.	Crushes paper into ball			
3.	Picks up tiny objects			
4.	Buttons shirts			
5.	Draws in wet sand			
6.	Opens and closes the door			
7.	Builds tower with building blocks			
8.	Rolls clay into balls			

A	PERFECT DEMONSTRATION OF SKILL	B	PROGRESSING TOWARDS SKILL	C	NEEDS IMPROVEMENT

SKILLS AND COMPETENCIES

LISTENING AND SPEAKING SKILLS		A	B	C
1.	Recognises sounds and rhymes			
2.	Follows instructions			
3.	Asks and answers questions			
4.	Listen to stories			
5.	Speaks clearly			
6.	Repeats rhymes with actions			
7.	Tells stories using pictures			
8.	Describes experiences			

WRITING AND CREATIVE SKILLS		A	B	C
1.	Traces patterns, letters and objects			
2.	Fills colours			
3.	Writes letters and words			
4.	Writes missing letters			
5.	Draws and matches objects			
6.	Makes models by using clay & paper			
7.	Predicts what comes next			
8.	Solving easy puzzles & problems			

A	PERFECT DEMONSTRATION OF SKILL	B	PROGRESSING TOWARDS SKILL	C	NEEDS IMPROVEMENT

SKILLS AND COMPETENCIES

LIFE SKILLS		A	B	C
1.	Hand and eye coordination			
2.	Eats on his or her own			
3.	Ask for help if needed			
4.	Sharing with others			
5.	Expresses likes and dislikes			
6.	Shows gratitude and thanks			
7.	Shows respect and kindness to elders			
8.	Cares for others, animals and plants			

VISUAL & DISCRIMINATION SKILLS		A	B	C
1.	Identifies objects, pictures & persons			
2.	Finds the object or person in the pic			
3.	Sorts objects of same size & colour			
4.	Matches objects			
5.	Finds the odd one out			
6.	Understands the position & direction			
7.	Identifies the shapes, colours & size			
8.	Understand the distance			

Teacher's Signature	

A	PERFECT DEMONSTRATION OF SKILL	B	PROGRESSING TOWARDS SKILL	C	NEEDS IMPROVEMENT

PHYSICAL DEVELOPMENT

GROSS MOTOR SKILLS	A	B	C
1. Walks with proper balance			
2. Hops on one foot			
3. Jumps			
4. Catches and throws a ball			
5. Steps over circles			
6. Marches with swinging arms			
7. Skips			
8. Balances on one foot			

FINE MOTOR SKILLS	A	B	C
1. Tears newspaper into strips			
2. Crushes paper into ball			
3. Picks up tiny objects			
4. Buttons shirts			
5. Draws in wet sand			
6. Opens and closes the door			
7. Builds tower with building blocks			
8. Rolls clay into balls			

A	PERFECT DEMONSTRATION OF SKILL	B	PROGRESSING TOWARDS SKILL	C	NEEDS IMPROVEMENT

SKILLS AND COMPETENCIES

LISTENING AND SPEAKING SKILLS	A	B	C
1. Recognises sounds and rhymes			
2. Follows instructions			
3. Asks and answers questions			
4. Listen to stories			
5. Speaks clearly			
6. Repeats rhymes with actions			
7. Tells stories using pictures			
8. Describes experiences			

WRITING AND CREATIVE SKILLS	A	B	C
1. Traces patterns, letters and objects			
2. Fills colours			
3. Writes letters and words			
4. Writes missing letters			
5. Draws and matches objects			
6. Makes models by using clay & paper			
7. Predicts what comes next			
8. Solving easy puzzles & problems			

A	PERFECT DEMONSTRATION OF SKILL	B	PROGRESSING TOWARDS SKILL	C	NEEDS IMPROVEMENT

SKILLS AND COMPETENCIES

	LIFE SKILLS	A	B	C
1.	Hand and eye coordination			
2.	Eats on his or her own			
3.	Ask for help if needed			
4.	Sharing with others			
5.	Expresses likes and dislikes			
6.	Shows gratitude and thanks			
7.	Shows respect and kindness to elders			
8.	Cares for others, animals and plants			

	VISUAL & DISCRIMINATION SKILLS	A	B	C
1.	Identifies objects, pictures & persons			
2.	Finds the object or person in the pic			
3.	Sorts objects of same size & colour			
4.	Matches objects			
5.	Finds the odd one out			
6.	Understands the position & direction			
7.	Identifies the shapes, colours & size			
8.	Understand the distance			

Teacher's Signature	

A	PERFECT DEMONSTRATION OF SKILL	**B**	PROGRESSING TOWARDS SKILL	**C**	NEEDS IMPROVEMENT

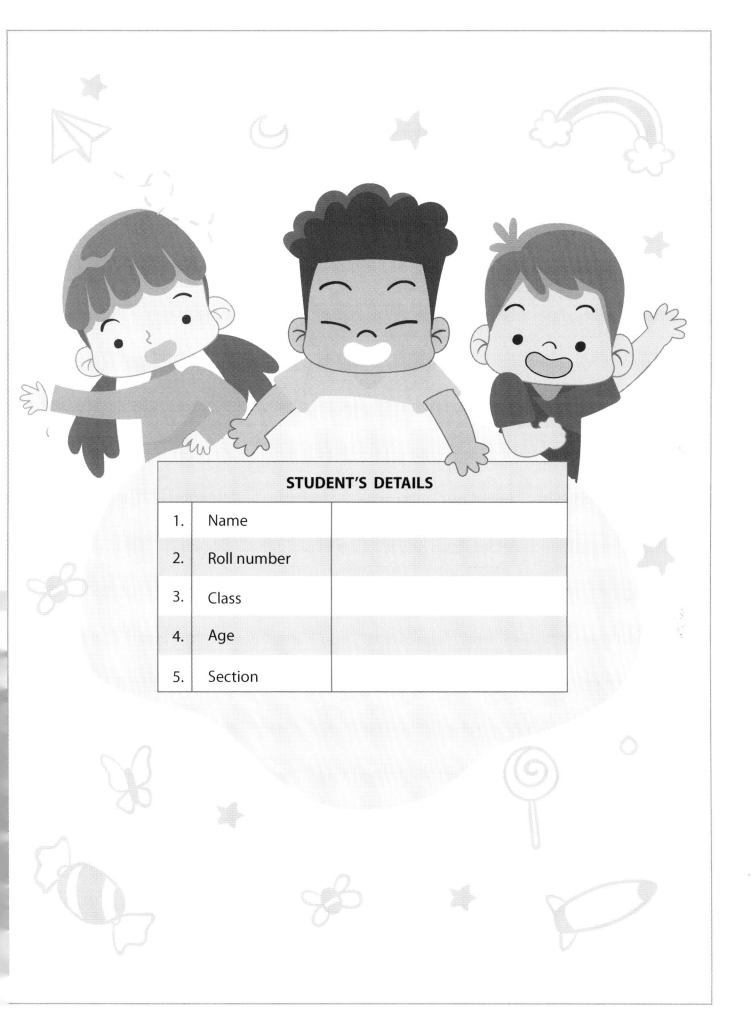

STUDENT'S DETAILS

1.	Name	
2.	Roll number	
3.	Class	
4.	Age	
5.	Section	

PHYSICAL DEVELOPMENT

GROSS MOTOR SKILLS	A	B	C
1. Walks with proper balance			
2. Hops on one foot			
3. Jumps			
4. Catches and throws a ball			
5. Steps over circles			
6. Marches with swinging arms			
7. Skips			
8. Balances on one foot			

FINE MOTOR SKILLS	A	B	C
1. Tears newspaper into strips			
2. Crushes paper into ball			
3. Picks up tiny objects			
4. Buttons shirts			
5. Draws in wet sand			
6. Opens and closes the door			
7. Builds tower with building blocks			
8. Rolls clay into balls			

A	PERFECT DEMONSTRATION OF SKILL	B	PROGRESSING TOWARDS SKILL	C	NEEDS IMPROVEMENT

SKILLS AND COMPETENCIES

LISTENING AND SPEAKING SKILLS		A	B	C
1.	Recognises sounds and rhymes			
2.	Follows instructions			
3.	Asks and answers questions			
4.	Listen to stories			
5.	Speaks clearly			
6.	Repeats rhymes with actions			
7.	Tells stories using pictures			
8.	Describes experiences			

WRITING AND CREATIVE SKILLS		A	B	C
1.	Traces patterns, letters and objects			
2.	Fills colours			
3.	Writes letters and words			
4.	Writes missing letters			
5.	Draws and matches objects			
6.	Makes models by using clay & paper			
7.	Predicts what comes next			
8.	Solving easy puzzles & problems			

A	PERFECT DEMONSTRATION OF SKILL	B	PROGRESSING TOWARDS SKILL	C	NEEDS IMPROVEMENT

SKILLS AND COMPETENCIES

LIFE SKILLS		A	B	C
1.	Hand and eye coordination			
2.	Eats on his or her own			
3.	Ask for help if needed			
4.	Sharing with others			
5.	Expresses likes and dislikes			
6.	Shows gratitude and thanks			
7.	Shows respect and kindness to elders			
8.	Cares for others, animals and plants			

VISUAL & DISCRIMINATION SKILLS		A	B	C
1.	Identifies objects, pictures & persons			
2.	Finds the object or person in the pic			
3.	Sorts objects of same size & colour			
4.	Matches objects			
5.	Finds the odd one out			
6.	Understands the position & direction			
7.	Identifies the shapes, colours & size			
8.	Understand the distance			

Teacher's Signature	

A	PERFECT DEMONSTRATION OF SKILL	B	PROGRESSING TOWARDS SKILL	C	NEEDS IMPROVEMENT

PHYSICAL DEVELOPMENT

GROSS MOTOR SKILLS		A	B	C
1.	Walks with proper balance			
2.	Hops on one foot			
3.	Jumps			
4.	Catches and throws a ball			
5.	Steps over circles			
6.	Marches with swinging arms			
7.	Skips			
8.	Balances on one foot			

FINE MOTOR SKILLS		A	B	C
1.	Tears newspaper into strips			
2.	Crushes paper into ball			
3.	Picks up tiny objects			
4.	Buttons shirts			
5.	Draws in wet sand			
6.	Opens and closes the door			
7.	Builds tower with building blocks			
8.	Rolls clay into balls			

A	PERFECT DEMONSTRATION OF SKILL	B	PROGRESSING TOWARDS SKILL	C	NEEDS IMPROVEMENT

ASSESSMENT - 2

NAME : _____

SKILLS AND COMPETENCIES

LISTENING AND SPEAKING SKILLS		A	B	C
1.	Recognises sounds and rhymes			
2.	Follows instructions			
3.	Asks and answers questions			
4.	Listen to stories			
5.	Speaks clearly			
6.	Repeats rhymes with actions			
7.	Tells stories using pictures			
8.	Describes experiences			

WRITING AND CREATIVE SKILLS		A	B	C
1.	Traces patterns, letters and objects			
2.	Fills colours			
3.	Writes letters and words			
4.	Writes missing letters			
5.	Draws and matches objects			
6.	Makes models by using clay & paper			
7.	Predicts what comes next			
8.	Solving easy puzzles & problems			

A PERFECT DEMONSTRATION OF SKILL	**B** PROGRESSING TOWARDS SKILL	**C** NEEDS IMPROVEMENT

SKILLS AND COMPETENCIES

LIFE SKILLS		A	B	C
1.	Hand and eye coordination			
2.	Eats on his or her own			
3.	Ask for help if needed			
4.	Sharing with others			
5.	Expresses likes and dislikes			
6.	Shows gratitude and thanks			
7.	Shows respect and kindness to elders			
8.	Cares for others, animals and plants			

VISUAL & DISCRIMINATION SKILLS		A	B	C
1.	Identifies objects, pictures & persons			
2.	Finds the object or person in the pic			
3.	Sorts objects of same size & colour			
4.	Matches objects			
5.	Finds the odd one out			
6.	Understands the position & direction			
7.	Identifies the shapes, colours & size			
8.	Understand the distance			

Teacher's Signature	

A	PERFECT DEMONSTRATION OF SKILL	B	PROGRESSING TOWARDS SKILL	C	NEEDS IMPROVEMENT

NAME : _____

PHYSICAL DEVELOPMENT

GROSS MOTOR SKILLS		A	B	C
1.	Walks with proper balance			
2.	Hops on one foot			
3.	Jumps			
4.	Catches and throws a ball			
5.	Steps over circles			
6.	Marches with swinging arms			
7.	Skips			
8.	Balances on one foot			

FINE MOTOR SKILLS		A	B	C
1.	Tears newspaper into strips			
2.	Crushes paper into ball			
3.	Picks up tiny objects			
4.	Buttons shirts			
5.	Draws in wet sand			
6.	Opens and closes the door			
7.	Builds tower with building blocks			
8.	Rolls clay into balls			

A	PERFECT DEMONSTRATION OF SKILL	B	PROGRESSING TOWARDS SKILL	C	NEEDS IMPROVEMENT

SKILLS AND COMPETENCIES

LISTENING AND SPEAKING SKILLS	A	B	C
1. Recognises sounds and rhymes			
2. Follows instructions			
3. Asks and answers questions			
4. Listen to stories			
5. Speaks clearly			
6. Repeats rhymes with actions			
7. Tells stories using pictures			
8. Describes experiences			

WRITING AND CREATIVE SKILLS	A	B	C
1. Traces patterns, letters and objects			
2. Fills colours			
3. Writes letters and words			
4. Writes missing letters			
5. Draws and matches objects			
6. Makes models by using clay & paper			
7. Predicts what comes next			
8. Solving easy puzzles & problems			

A PERFECT DEMONSTRATION OF SKILL   **B** PROGRESSING TOWARDS SKILL   **C** NEEDS IMPROVEMENT

NAME : _____

SKILLS AND COMPETENCIES

	LIFE SKILLS	A	B	C
1.	Hand and eye coordination			
2.	Eats on his or her own			
3.	Ask for help if needed			
4.	Sharing with others			
5.	Expresses likes and dislikes			
6.	Shows gratitude and thanks			
7.	Shows respect and kindness to elders			
8.	Cares for others, animals and plants			

	VISUAL & DISCRIMINATION SKILLS	A	B	C
1.	Identifies objects, pictures & persons			
2.	Finds the object or person in the pic			
3.	Sorts objects of same size & colour			
4.	Matches objects			
5.	Finds the odd one out			
6.	Understands the position & direction			
7.	Identifies the shapes, colours & size			
8.	Understand the distance			

Teacher's Signature	

A	PERFECT DEMONSTRATION OF SKILL	**B**	PROGRESSING TOWARDS SKILL	**C**	NEEDS IMPROVEMENT

STUDENT'S DETAILS

1.	Name	
2.	Roll number	
3.	Class	
4.	Age	
5.	Section	

ASSESSMENT - 1   NAME : _____

PHYSICAL DEVELOPMENT

GROSS MOTOR SKILLS	A	B	C
1. Walks with proper balance			
2. Hops on one foot			
3. Jumps			
4. Catches and throws a ball			
5. Steps over circles			
6. Marches with swinging arms			
7. Skips			
8. Balances on one foot			

FINE MOTOR SKILLS	A	B	C
1. Tears newspaper into strips			
2. Crushes paper into ball			
3. Picks up tiny objects			
4. Buttons shirts			
5. Draws in wet sand			
6. Opens and closes the door			
7. Builds tower with building blocks			
8. Rolls clay into balls			

A PERFECT DEMONSTRATION OF SKILL **B** PROGRESSING TOWARDS SKILL **C** NEEDS IMPROVEMENT

SKILLS AND COMPETENCIES

LISTENING AND SPEAKING SKILLS	A	B	C
1.	Recognises sounds and rhymes			
2.	Follows instructions			
3.	Asks and answers questions			
4.	Listen to stories			
5.	Speaks clearly			
6.	Repeats rhymes with actions			
7.	Tells stories using pictures			
8.	Describes experiences			

WRITING AND CREATIVE SKILLS	A	B	C
1.	Traces patterns, letters and objects			
2.	Fills colours			
3.	Writes letters and words			
4.	Writes missing letters			
5.	Draws and matches objects			
6.	Makes models by using clay & paper			
7.	Predicts what comes next			
8.	Solving easy puzzles & problems			

A	PERFECT DEMONSTRATION OF SKILL	B	PROGRESSING TOWARDS SKILL	C	NEEDS IMPROVEMENT

SKILLS AND COMPETENCIES

LIFE SKILLS		A	B	C
1.	Hand and eye coordination			
2.	Eats on his or her own			
3.	Ask for help if needed			
4.	Sharing with others			
5.	Expresses likes and dislikes			
6.	Shows gratitude and thanks			
7.	Shows respect and kindness to elders			
8.	Cares for others, animals and plants			

VISUAL & DISCRIMINATION SKILLS		A	B	C
1.	Identifies objects, pictures & persons			
2.	Finds the object or person in the pic			
3.	Sorts objects of same size & colour			
4.	Matches objects			
5.	Finds the odd one out			
6.	Understands the position & direction			
7.	Identifies the shapes, colours & size			
8.	Understand the distance			

Teacher's Signature	

A	PERFECT DEMONSTRATION OF SKILL	**B**	PROGRESSING TOWARDS SKILL	**C**	NEEDS IMPROVEMENT

PHYSICAL DEVELOPMENT

GROSS MOTOR SKILLS	A	B	C
1. Walks with proper balance			
2. Hops on one foot			
3. Jumps			
4. Catches and throws a ball			
5. Steps over circles			
6. Marches with swinging arms			
7. Skips			
8. Balances on one foot			

FINE MOTOR SKILLS	A	B	C
1. Tears newspaper into strips			
2. Crushes paper into ball			
3. Picks up tiny objects			
4. Buttons shirts			
5. Draws in wet sand			
6. Opens and closes the door			
7. Builds tower with building blocks			
8. Rolls clay into balls			

A	PERFECT DEMONSTRATION OF SKILL	B	PROGRESSING TOWARDS SKILL	C	NEEDS IMPROVEMENT

ASSESSMENT - 2

NAME : _____

SKILLS AND COMPETENCIES

LISTENING AND SPEAKING SKILLS		A	B	C
1.	Recognises sounds and rhymes			
2.	Follows instructions			
3.	Asks and answers questions			
4.	Listen to stories			
5.	Speaks clearly			
6.	Repeats rhymes with actions			
7.	Tells stories using pictures			
8.	Describes experiences			

WRITING AND CREATIVE SKILLS		A	B	C
1.	Traces patterns, letters and objects			
2.	Fills colours			
3.	Writes letters and words			
4.	Writes missing letters			
5.	Draws and matches objects			
6.	Makes models by using clay & paper			
7.	Predicts what comes next			
8.	Solving easy puzzles & problems			

A PERFECT DEMONSTRATION OF SKILL	**B** PROGRESSING TOWARDS SKILL	**C** NEEDS IMPROVEMENT

SKILLS AND COMPETENCIES

	LIFE SKILLS	A	B	C
1.	Hand and eye coordination			
2.	Eats on his or her own			
3.	Ask for help if needed			
4.	Sharing with others			
5.	Expresses likes and dislikes			
6.	Shows gratitude and thanks			
7.	Shows respect and kindness to elders			
8.	Cares for others, animals and plants			

	VISUAL & DISCRIMINATION SKILLS	A	B	C
1.	Identifies objects, pictures & persons			
2.	Finds the object or person in the pic			
3.	Sorts objects of same size & colour			
4.	Matches objects			
5.	Finds the odd one out			
6.	Understands the position & direction			
7.	Identifies the shapes, colours & size			
8.	Understand the distance			

Teacher's Signature	

A	PERFECT DEMONSTRATION OF SKILL	B	PROGRESSING TOWARDS SKILL	C	NEEDS IMPROVEMENT

PHYSICAL DEVELOPMENT

GROSS MOTOR SKILLS		A	B	C
1.	Walks with proper balance			
2.	Hops on one foot			
3.	Jumps			
4.	Catches and throws a ball			
5.	Steps over circles			
6.	Marches with swinging arms			
7.	Skips			
8.	Balances on one foot			

FINE MOTOR SKILLS		A	B	C
1.	Tears newspaper into strips			
2.	Crushes paper into ball			
3.	Picks up tiny objects			
4.	Buttons shirts			
5.	Draws in wet sand			
6.	Opens and closes the door			
7.	Builds tower with building blocks			
8.	Rolls clay into balls			

A	PERFECT DEMONSTRATION OF SKILL	B	PROGRESSING TOWARDS SKILL	C	NEEDS IMPROVEMENT

SKILLS AND COMPETENCIES

LISTENING AND SPEAKING SKILLS		A	B	C
1.	Recognises sounds and rhymes			
2.	Follows instructions			
3.	Asks and answers questions			
4.	Listen to stories			
5.	Speaks clearly			
6.	Repeats rhymes with actions			
7.	Tells stories using pictures			
8.	Describes experiences			

WRITING AND CREATIVE SKILLS		A	B	C
1.	Traces patterns, letters and objects			
2.	Fills colours			
3.	Writes letters and words			
4.	Writes missing letters			
5.	Draws and matches objects			
6.	Makes models by using clay & paper			
7.	Predicts what comes next			
8.	Solving easy puzzles & problems			

A	PERFECT DEMONSTRATION OF SKILL	B	PROGRESSING TOWARDS SKILL	C	NEEDS IMPROVEMENT

SKILLS AND COMPETENCIES

	LIFE SKILLS	A	B	C
1.	Hand and eye coordination			
2.	Eats on his or her own			
3.	Ask for help if needed			
4.	Sharing with others			
5.	Expresses likes and dislikes			
6.	Shows gratitude and thanks			
7.	Shows respect and kindness to elders			
8.	Cares for others, animals and plants			

	VISUAL & DISCRIMINATION SKILLS	A	B	C
1.	Identifies objects, pictures & persons			
2.	Finds the object or person in the pic			
3.	Sorts objects of same size & colour			
4.	Matches objects			
5.	Finds the odd one out			
6.	Understands the position & direction			
7.	Identifies the shapes, colours & size			
8.	Understand the distance			

Teacher's Signature	

A	PERFECT DEMONSTRATION OF SKILL	**B**	PROGRESSING TOWARDS SKILL	**C**	NEEDS IMPROVEMENT

STUDENT'S DETAILS

1.	Name	
2.	Roll number	
3.	Class	
4.	Age	
5.	Section	

PHYSICAL DEVELOPMENT

GROSS MOTOR SKILLS		A	B	C
1.	Walks with proper balance			
2.	Hops on one foot			
3.	Jumps			
4.	Catches and throws a ball			
5.	Steps over circles			
6.	Marches with swinging arms			
7.	Skips			
8.	Balances on one foot			

FINE MOTOR SKILLS		A	B	C
1.	Tears newspaper into strips			
2.	Crushes paper into ball			
3.	Picks up tiny objects			
4.	Buttons shirts			
5.	Draws in wet sand			
6.	Opens and closes the door			
7.	Builds tower with building blocks			
8.	Rolls clay into balls			

A	PERFECT DEMONSTRATION OF SKILL	B	PROGRESSING TOWARDS SKILL	C	NEEDS IMPROVEMENT

SKILLS AND COMPETENCIES

LISTENING AND SPEAKING SKILLS	A	B	C
1. Recognises sounds and rhymes			
2. Follows instructions			
3. Asks and answers questions			
4. Listen to stories			
5. Speaks clearly			
6. Repeats rhymes with actions			
7. Tells stories using pictures			
8. Describes experiences			

WRITING AND CREATIVE SKILLS	A	B	C
1. Traces patterns, letters and objects			
2. Fills colours			
3. Writes letters and words			
4. Writes missing letters			
5. Draws and matches objects			
6. Makes models by using clay & paper			
7. Predicts what comes next			
8. Solving easy puzzles & problems			

A	PERFECT DEMONSTRATION OF SKILL	B	PROGRESSING TOWARDS SKILL	C	NEEDS IMPROVEMENT

NAME : _____

SKILLS AND COMPETENCIES

LIFE SKILLS		A	B	C
1.	Hand and eye coordination			
2.	Eats on his or her own			
3.	Ask for help if needed			
4.	Sharing with others			
5.	Expresses likes and dislikes			
6.	Shows gratitude and thanks			
7.	Shows respect and kindness to elders			
8.	Cares for others, animals and plants			

VISUAL & DISCRIMINATION SKILLS		A	B	C
1.	Identifies objects, pictures & persons			
2.	Finds the object or person in the pic			
3.	Sorts objects of same size & colour			
4.	Matches objects			
5.	Finds the odd one out			
6.	Understands the position & direction			
7.	Identifies the shapes, colours & size			
8.	Understand the distance			

Teacher's Signature	

A	PERFECT DEMONSTRATION OF SKILL	**B**	PROGRESSING TOWARDS SKILL	**C**	NEEDS IMPROVEMENT

PHYSICAL DEVELOPMENT

GROSS MOTOR SKILLS		A	B	C
1.	Walks with proper balance			
2.	Hops on one foot			
3.	Jumps			
4.	Catches and throws a ball			
5.	Steps over circles			
6.	Marches with swinging arms			
7.	Skips			
8.	Balances on one foot			

FINE MOTOR SKILLS		A	B	C
1.	Tears newspaper into strips			
2.	Crushes paper into ball			
3.	Picks up tiny objects			
4.	Buttons shirts			
5.	Draws in wet sand			
6.	Opens and closes the door			
7.	Builds tower with building blocks			
8.	Rolls clay into balls			

A	PERFECT DEMONSTRATION OF SKILL	B	PROGRESSING TOWARDS SKILL	C	NEEDS IMPROVEMENT

SKILLS AND COMPETENCIES

LISTENING AND SPEAKING SKILLS	A	B	C
1. Recognises sounds and rhymes			
2. Follows instructions			
3. Asks and answers questions			
4. Listen to stories			
5. Speaks clearly			
6. Repeats rhymes with actions			
7. Tells stories using pictures			
8. Describes experiences			

WRITING AND CREATIVE SKILLS	A	B	C
1. Traces patterns, letters and objects			
2. Fills colours			
3. Writes letters and words			
4. Writes missing letters			
5. Draws and matches objects			
6. Makes models by using clay & paper			
7. Predicts what comes next			
8. Solving easy puzzles & problems			

A	PERFECT DEMONSTRATION OF SKILL	B	PROGRESSING TOWARDS SKILL	C	NEEDS IMPROVEMENT

SKILLS AND COMPETENCIES

LIFE SKILLS		A	B	C
1.	Hand and eye coordination			
2.	Eats on his or her own			
3.	Ask for help if needed			
4.	Sharing with others			
5.	Expresses likes and dislikes			
6.	Shows gratitude and thanks			
7.	Shows respect and kindness to elders			
8.	Cares for others, animals and plants			

VISUAL & DISCRIMINATION SKILLS		A	B	C
1.	Identifies objects, pictures & persons			
2.	Finds the object or person in the pic			
3.	Sorts objects of same size & colour			
4.	Matches objects			
5.	Finds the odd one out			
6.	Understands the position & direction			
7.	Identifies the shapes, colours & size			
8.	Understand the distance			

Teacher's Signature	

A	PERFECT DEMONSTRATION OF SKILL	**B**	PROGRESSING TOWARDS SKILL	**C**	NEEDS IMPROVEMENT

ASSESSMENT - 3

NAME : _____

PHYSICAL DEVELOPMENT

GROSS MOTOR SKILLS		A	B	C
1.	Walks with proper balance			
2.	Hops on one foot			
3.	Jumps			
4.	Catches and throws a ball			
5.	Steps over circles			
6.	Marches with swinging arms			
7.	Skips			
8.	Balances on one foot			

FINE MOTOR SKILLS		A	B	C
1.	Tears newspaper into strips			
2.	Crushes paper into ball			
3.	Picks up tiny objects			
4.	Buttons shirts			
5.	Draws in wet sand			
6.	Opens and closes the door			
7.	Builds tower with building blocks			
8.	Rolls clay into balls			

| A | PERFECT DEMONSTRATION OF SKILL | B | PROGRESSING TOWARDS SKILL | C | NEEDS IMPROVEMENT |

SKILLS AND COMPETENCIES

LISTENING AND SPEAKING SKILLS	A	B	C
1. Recognises sounds and rhymes			
2. Follows instructions			
3. Asks and answers questions			
4. Listen to stories			
5. Speaks clearly			
6. Repeats rhymes with actions			
7. Tells stories using pictures			
8. Describes experiences			

WRITING AND CREATIVE SKILLS	A	B	C
1. Traces patterns, letters and objects			
2. Fills colours			
3. Writes letters and words			
4. Writes missing letters			
5. Draws and matches objects			
6. Makes models by using clay & paper			
7. Predicts what comes next			
8. Solving easy puzzles & problems			

A	PERFECT DEMONSTRATION OF SKILL	B	PROGRESSING TOWARDS SKILL	C	NEEDS IMPROVEMENT

SKILLS AND COMPETENCIES

	LIFE SKILLS	A	B	C
1.	Hand and eye coordination			
2.	Eats on his or her own			
3.	Ask for help if needed			
4.	Sharing with others			
5.	Expresses likes and dislikes			
6.	Shows gratitude and thanks			
7.	Shows respect and kindness to elders			
8.	Cares for others, animals and plants			

	VISUAL & DISCRIMINATION SKILLS	A	B	C
1.	Identifies objects, pictures & persons			
2.	Finds the object or person in the pic			
3.	Sorts objects of same size & colour			
4.	Matches objects			
5.	Finds the odd one out			
6.	Understands the position & direction			
7.	Identifies the shapes, colours & size			
8.	Understand the distance			

Teacher's Signature	

A	PERFECT DEMONSTRATION OF SKILL	**B**	PROGRESSING TOWARDS SKILL	**C**	NEEDS IMPROVEMENT

STUDENT'S DETAILS

1.	Name	
2.	Roll number	
3.	Class	
4.	Age	
5.	Section	

PHYSICAL DEVELOPMENT

	GROSS MOTOR SKILLS	A	B	C
1.	Walks with proper balance			
2.	Hops on one foot			
3.	Jumps			
4.	Catches and throws a ball			
5.	Steps over circles			
6.	Marches with swinging arms			
7.	Skips			
8.	Balances on one foot			

	FINE MOTOR SKILLS	A	B	C
1.	Tears newspaper into strips			
2.	Crushes paper into ball			
3.	Picks up tiny objects			
4.	Buttons shirts			
5.	Draws in wet sand			
6.	Opens and closes the door			
7.	Builds tower with building blocks			
8.	Rolls clay into balls			

A PERFECT DEMONSTRATION OF SKILL	**B** PROGRESSING TOWARDS SKILL	**C** NEEDS IMPROVEMENT

NAME : _____

SKILLS AND COMPETENCIES

LISTENING AND SPEAKING SKILLS	A	B	C
1. Recognises sounds and rhymes			
2. Follows instructions			
3. Asks and answers questions			
4. Listen to stories			
5. Speaks clearly			
6. Repeats rhymes with actions			
7. Tells stories using pictures			
8. Describes experiences			

WRITING AND CREATIVE SKILLS	A	B	C
1. Traces patterns, letters and objects			
2. Fills colours			
3. Writes letters and words			
4. Writes missing letters			
5. Draws and matches objects			
6. Makes models by using clay & paper			
7. Predicts what comes next			
8. Solving easy puzzles & problems			

A	PERFECT DEMONSTRATION OF SKILL	B	PROGRESSING TOWARDS SKILL	C	NEEDS IMPROVEMENT

SKILLS AND COMPETENCIES

	LIFE SKILLS	A	B	C
1.	Hand and eye coordination			
2.	Eats on his or her own			
3.	Ask for help if needed			
4.	Sharing with others			
5.	Expresses likes and dislikes			
6.	Shows gratitude and thanks			
7.	Shows respect and kindness to elders			
8.	Cares for others, animals and plants			

	VISUAL & DISCRIMINATION SKILLS	A	B	C
1.	Identifies objects, pictures & persons			
2.	Finds the object or person in the pic			
3.	Sorts objects of same size & colour			
4.	Matches objects			
5.	Finds the odd one out			
6.	Understands the position & direction			
7.	Identifies the shapes, colours & size			
8.	Understand the distance			

Teacher's Signature	

A	PERFECT DEMONSTRATION OF SKILL	B	PROGRESSING TOWARDS SKILL	C	NEEDS IMPROVEMENT

　　　　　　NAME : _____

PHYSICAL DEVELOPMENT

GROSS MOTOR SKILLS		A	B	C
1.	Walks with proper balance			
2.	Hops on one foot			
3.	Jumps			
4.	Catches and throws a ball			
5.	Steps over circles			
6.	Marches with swinging arms			
7.	Skips			
8.	Balances on one foot			

FINE MOTOR SKILLS		A	B	C
1.	Tears newspaper into strips			
2.	Crushes paper into ball			
3.	Picks up tiny objects			
4.	Buttons shirts			
5.	Draws in wet sand			
6.	Opens and closes the door			
7.	Builds tower with building blocks			
8.	Rolls clay into balls			

A	PERFECT DEMONSTRATION OF SKILL	B	PROGRESSING TOWARDS SKILL	C	NEEDS IMPROVEMENT

ASSESSMENT - 2

NAME : _____

SKILLS AND COMPETENCIES

LISTENING AND SPEAKING SKILLS		A	B	C
1.	Recognises sounds and rhymes			
2.	Follows instructions			
3.	Asks and answers questions			
4.	Listen to stories			
5.	Speaks clearly			
6.	Repeats rhymes with actions			
7.	Tells stories using pictures			
8.	Describes experiences			

WRITING AND CREATIVE SKILLS		A	B	C
1.	Traces patterns, letters and objects			
2.	Fills colours			
3.	Writes letters and words			
4.	Writes missing letters			
5.	Draws and matches objects			
6.	Makes models by using clay & paper			
7.	Predicts what comes next			
8.	Solving easy puzzles & problems			

A	PERFECT DEMONSTRATION OF SKILL	B	PROGRESSING TOWARDS SKILL	C	NEEDS IMPROVEMENT

ASSESSMENT - 2   NAME : _____

SKILLS AND COMPETENCIES

	LIFE SKILLS	A	B	C
1.	Hand and eye coordination			
2.	Eats on his or her own			
3.	Ask for help if needed			
4.	Sharing with others			
5.	Expresses likes and dislikes			
6.	Shows gratitude and thanks			
7.	Shows respect and kindness to elders			
8.	Cares for others, animals and plants			

	VISUAL & DISCRIMINATION SKILLS	A	B	C
1.	Identifies objects, pictures & persons			
2.	Finds the object or person in the pic			
3.	Sorts objects of same size & colour			
4.	Matches objects			
5.	Finds the odd one out			
6.	Understands the position & direction			
7.	Identifies the shapes, colours & size			
8.	Understand the distance			

Teacher's Signature	

A	PERFECT DEMONSTRATION OF SKILL	**B**	PROGRESSING TOWARDS SKILL	**C**	NEEDS IMPROVEMENT

NAME : _____

PHYSICAL DEVELOPMENT

GROSS MOTOR SKILLS		A	B	C
1.	Walks with proper balance			
2.	Hops on one foot			
3.	Jumps			
4.	Catches and throws a ball			
5.	Steps over circles			
6.	Marches with swinging arms			
7.	Skips			
8.	Balances on one foot			

FINE MOTOR SKILLS		A	B	C
1.	Tears newspaper into strips			
2.	Crushes paper into ball			
3.	Picks up tiny objects			
4.	Buttons shirts			
5.	Draws in wet sand			
6.	Opens and closes the door			
7.	Builds tower with building blocks			
8.	Rolls clay into balls			

A	PERFECT DEMONSTRATION OF SKILL	B	PROGRESSING TOWARDS SKILL	C	NEEDS IMPROVEMENT

SKILLS AND COMPETENCIES

LISTENING AND SPEAKING SKILLS	A	B	C
1.	Recognises sounds and rhymes			
2.	Follows instructions			
3.	Asks and answers questions			
4.	Listen to stories			
5.	Speaks clearly			
6.	Repeats rhymes with actions			
7.	Tells stories using pictures			
8.	Describes experiences			

WRITING AND CREATIVE SKILLS	A	B	C
1.	Traces patterns, letters and objects			
2.	Fills colours			
3.	Writes letters and words			
4.	Writes missing letters			
5.	Draws and matches objects			
6.	Makes models by using clay & paper			
7.	Predicts what comes next			
8.	Solving easy puzzles & problems			

A	PERFECT DEMONSTRATION OF SKILL	B	PROGRESSING TOWARDS SKILL	C	NEEDS IMPROVEMENT

ASSESSMENT - 3   NAME : _____

SKILLS AND COMPETENCIES

LIFE SKILLS	A	B	C
1. Hand and eye coordination			
2. Eats on his or her own			
3. Ask for help if needed			
4. Sharing with others			
5. Expresses likes and dislikes			
6. Shows gratitude and thanks			
7. Shows respect and kindness to elders			
8. Cares for others, animals and plants			

VISUAL & DISCRIMINATION SKILLS	A	B	C
1. Identifies objects, pictures & persons			
2. Finds the object or person in the pic			
3. Sorts objects of same size & colour			
4. Matches objects			
5. Finds the odd one out			
6. Understands the position & direction			
7. Identifies the shapes, colours & size			
8. Understand the distance			

Teacher's Signature	

A PERFECT DEMONSTRATION OF SKILL   **B** PROGRESSING TOWARDS SKILL   **C** NEEDS IMPROVEMENT

STUDENT'S DETAILS

1.	Name	
2.	Roll number	
3.	Class	
4.	Age	
5.	Section	

PHYSICAL DEVELOPMENT

GROSS MOTOR SKILLS	A	B	C
1. Walks with proper balance			
2. Hops on one foot			
3. Jumps			
4. Catches and throws a ball			
5. Steps over circles			
6. Marches with swinging arms			
7. Skips			
8. Balances on one foot			

FINE MOTOR SKILLS	A	B	C
1. Tears newspaper into strips			
2. Crushes paper into ball			
3. Picks up tiny objects			
4. Buttons shirts			
5. Draws in wet sand			
6. Opens and closes the door			
7. Builds tower with building blocks			
8. Rolls clay into balls			

A	PERFECT DEMONSTRATION OF SKILL	B	PROGRESSING TOWARDS SKILL	C	NEEDS IMPROVEMENT

ASSESSMENT - 1

NAME : _____

SKILLS AND COMPETENCIES

LISTENING AND SPEAKING SKILLS		A	B	C
1.	Recognises sounds and rhymes			
2.	Follows instructions			
3.	Asks and answers questions			
4.	Listen to stories			
5.	Speaks clearly			
6.	Repeats rhymes with actions			
7.	Tells stories using pictures			
8.	Describes experiences			

WRITING AND CREATIVE SKILLS		A	B	C
1.	Traces patterns, letters and objects			
2.	Fills colours			
3.	Writes letters and words			
4.	Writes missing letters			
5.	Draws and matches objects			
6.	Makes models by using clay & paper			
7.	Predicts what comes next			
8.	Solving easy puzzles & problems			

A PERFECT DEMONSTRATION OF SKILL	**B** PROGRESSING TOWARDS SKILL	**C** NEEDS IMPROVEMENT

SKILLS AND COMPETENCIES

LIFE SKILLS		A	B	C
1.	Hand and eye coordination			
2.	Eats on his or her own			
3.	Ask for help if needed			
4.	Sharing with others			
5.	Expresses likes and dislikes			
6.	Shows gratitude and thanks			
7.	Shows respect and kindness to elders			
8.	Cares for others, animals and plants			

VISUAL & DISCRIMINATION SKILLS		A	B	C
1.	Identifies objects, pictures & persons			
2.	Finds the object or person in the pic			
3.	Sorts objects of same size & colour			
4.	Matches objects			
5.	Finds the odd one out			
6.	Understands the position & direction			
7.	Identifies the shapes, colours & size			
8.	Understand the distance			

Teacher's Signature	

A	PERFECT DEMONSTRATION OF SKILL	**B**	PROGRESSING TOWARDS SKILL	**C**	NEEDS IMPROVEMENT

PHYSICAL DEVELOPMENT

GROSS MOTOR SKILLS		A	B	C
1.	Walks with proper balance			
2.	Hops on one foot			
3.	Jumps			
4.	Catches and throws a ball			
5.	Steps over circles			
6.	Marches with swinging arms			
7.	Skips			
8.	Balances on one foot			

FINE MOTOR SKILLS		A	B	C
1.	Tears newspaper into strips			
2.	Crushes paper into ball			
3.	Picks up tiny objects			
4.	Buttons shirts			
5.	Draws in wet sand			
6.	Opens and closes the door			
7.	Builds tower with building blocks			
8.	Rolls clay into balls			

A	PERFECT DEMONSTRATION OF SKILL	B	PROGRESSING TOWARDS SKILL	C	NEEDS IMPROVEMENT

SKILLS AND COMPETENCIES

LISTENING AND SPEAKING SKILLS		A	B	C
1.	Recognises sounds and rhymes			
2.	Follows instructions			
3.	Asks and answers questions			
4.	Listen to stories			
5.	Speaks clearly			
6.	Repeats rhymes with actions			
7.	Tells stories using pictures			
8.	Describes experiences			

WRITING AND CREATIVE SKILLS		A	B	C
1.	Traces patterns, letters and objects			
2.	Fills colours			
3.	Writes letters and words			
4.	Writes missing letters			
5.	Draws and matches objects			
6.	Makes models by using clay & paper			
7.	Predicts what comes next			
8.	Solving easy puzzles & problems			

A	PERFECT DEMONSTRATION OF SKILL	B	PROGRESSING TOWARDS SKILL	C	NEEDS IMPROVEMENT

SKILLS AND COMPETENCIES

	LIFE SKILLS	A	B	C
1.	Hand and eye coordination			
2.	Eats on his or her own			
3.	Ask for help if needed			
4.	Sharing with others			
5.	Expresses likes and dislikes			
6.	Shows gratitude and thanks			
7.	Shows respect and kindness to elders			
8.	Cares for others, animals and plants			

	VISUAL & DISCRIMINATION SKILLS	A	B	C
1.	Identifies objects, pictures & persons			
2.	Finds the object or person in the pic			
3.	Sorts objects of same size & colour			
4.	Matches objects			
5.	Finds the odd one out			
6.	Understands the position & direction			
7.	Identifies the shapes, colours & size			
8.	Understand the distance			

Teacher's Signature	

A	PERFECT DEMONSTRATION OF SKILL	B	PROGRESSING TOWARDS SKILL	C	NEEDS IMPROVEMENT

PHYSICAL DEVELOPMENT

GROSS MOTOR SKILLS	A	B	C
1. Walks with proper balance			
2. Hops on one foot			
3. Jumps			
4. Catches and throws a ball			
5. Steps over circles			
6. Marches with swinging arms			
7. Skips			
8. Balances on one foot			

FINE MOTOR SKILLS	A	B	C
1. Tears newspaper into strips			
2. Crushes paper into ball			
3. Picks up tiny objects			
4. Buttons shirts			
5. Draws in wet sand			
6. Opens and closes the door			
7. Builds tower with building blocks			
8. Rolls clay into balls			

A PERFECT DEMONSTRATION OF SKILL   **B** PROGRESSING TOWARDS SKILL   **C** NEEDS IMPROVEMENT

SKILLS AND COMPETENCIES

LISTENING AND SPEAKING SKILLS	A	B	C
1. Recognises sounds and rhymes			
2. Follows instructions			
3. Asks and answers questions			
4. Listen to stories			
5. Speaks clearly			
6. Repeats rhymes with actions			
7. Tells stories using pictures			
8. Describes experiences			

WRITING AND CREATIVE SKILLS	A	B	C
1. Traces patterns, letters and objects			
2. Fills colours			
3. Writes letters and words			
4. Writes missing letters			
5. Draws and matches objects			
6. Makes models by using clay & paper			
7. Predicts what comes next			
8. Solving easy puzzles & problems			

A	PERFECT DEMONSTRATION OF SKILL	B	PROGRESSING TOWARDS SKILL	C	NEEDS IMPROVEMENT

NAME : _____

SKILLS AND COMPETENCIES

	LIFE SKILLS	A	B	C
1.	Hand and eye coordination			
2.	Eats on his or her own			
3.	Ask for help if needed			
4.	Sharing with others			
5.	Expresses likes and dislikes			
6.	Shows gratitude and thanks			
7.	Shows respect and kindness to elders			
8.	Cares for others, animals and plants			

	VISUAL & DISCRIMINATION SKILLS	A	B	C
1.	Identifies objects, pictures & persons			
2.	Finds the object or person in the pic			
3.	Sorts objects of same size & colour			
4.	Matches objects			
5.	Finds the odd one out			
6.	Understands the position & direction			
7.	Identifies the shapes, colours & size			
8.	Understand the distance			

Teacher's Signature	

A	PERFECT DEMONSTRATION OF SKILL	B	PROGRESSING TOWARDS SKILL	C	NEEDS IMPROVEMENT

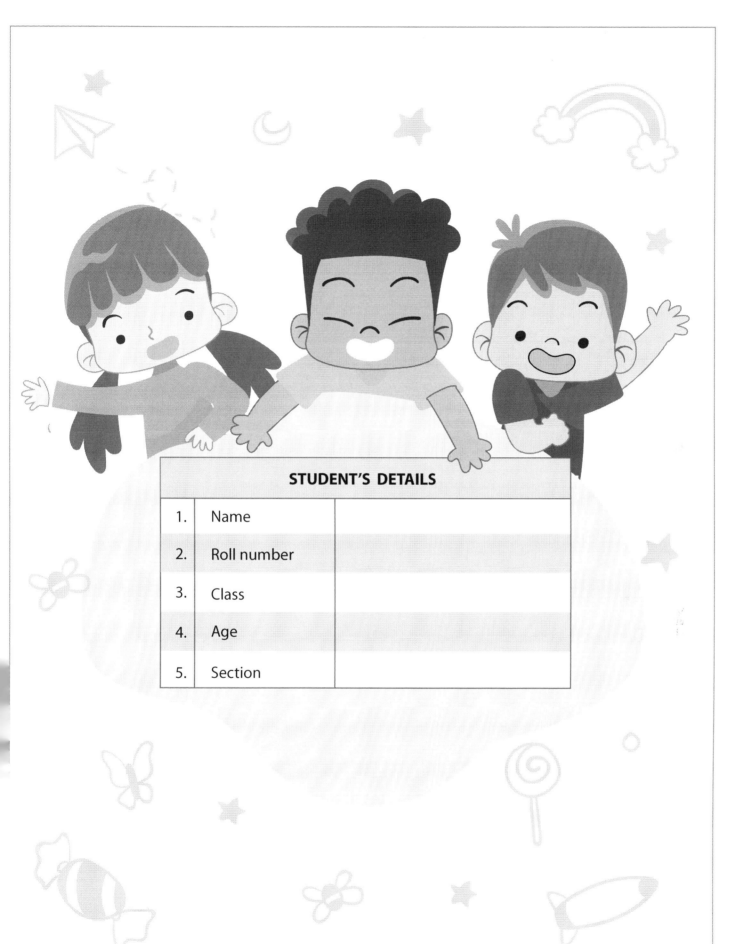

STUDENT'S DETAILS

1.	Name	
2.	Roll number	
3.	Class	
4.	Age	
5.	Section	

PHYSICAL DEVELOPMENT

	GROSS MOTOR SKILLS	A	B	C
1.	Walks with proper balance			
2.	Hops on one foot			
3.	Jumps			
4.	Catches and throws a ball			
5.	Steps over circles			
6.	Marches with swinging arms			
7.	Skips			
8.	Balances on one foot			

	FINE MOTOR SKILLS	A	B	C
1.	Tears newspaper into strips			
2.	Crushes paper into ball			
3.	Picks up tiny objects			
4.	Buttons shirts			
5.	Draws in wet sand			
6.	Opens and closes the door			
7.	Builds tower with building blocks			
8.	Rolls clay into balls			

A	PERFECT DEMONSTRATION OF SKILL	B	PROGRESSING TOWARDS SKILL	C	NEEDS IMPROVEMENT

SKILLS AND COMPETENCIES

LISTENING AND SPEAKING SKILLS		A	B	C
1.	Recognises sounds and rhymes			
2.	Follows instructions			
3.	Asks and answers questions			
4.	Listen to stories			
5.	Speaks clearly			
6.	Repeats rhymes with actions			
7.	Tells stories using pictures			
8.	Describes experiences			

WRITING AND CREATIVE SKILLS		A	B	C
1.	Traces patterns, letters and objects			
2.	Fills colours			
3.	Writes letters and words			
4.	Writes missing letters			
5.	Draws and matches objects			
6.	Makes models by using clay & paper			
7.	Predicts what comes next			
8.	Solving easy puzzles & problems			

A	PERFECT DEMONSTRATION OF SKILL	B	PROGRESSING TOWARDS SKILL	C	NEEDS IMPROVEMENT

SKILLS AND COMPETENCIES

LIFE SKILLS		A	B	C
1.	Hand and eye coordination			
2.	Eats on his or her own			
3.	Ask for help if needed			
4.	Sharing with others			
5.	Expresses likes and dislikes			
6.	Shows gratitude and thanks			
7.	Shows respect and kindness to elders			
8.	Cares for others, animals and plants			

VISUAL & DISCRIMINATION SKILLS		A	B	C
1.	Identifies objects, pictures & persons			
2.	Finds the object or person in the pic			
3.	Sorts objects of same size & colour			
4.	Matches objects			
5.	Finds the odd one out			
6.	Understands the position & direction			
7.	Identifies the shapes, colours & size			
8.	Understand the distance			

Teacher's Signature	

A	PERFECT DEMONSTRATION OF SKILL	**B**	PROGRESSING TOWARDS SKILL	**C**	NEEDS IMPROVEMENT

PHYSICAL DEVELOPMENT

GROSS MOTOR SKILLS		A	B	C
1.	Walks with proper balance			
2.	Hops on one foot			
3.	Jumps			
4.	Catches and throws a ball			
5.	Steps over circles			
6.	Marches with swinging arms			
7.	Skips			
8.	Balances on one foot			

FINE MOTOR SKILLS		A	B	C
1.	Tears newspaper into strips			
2.	Crushes paper into ball			
3.	Picks up tiny objects			
4.	Buttons shirts			
5.	Draws in wet sand			
6.	Opens and closes the door			
7.	Builds tower with building blocks			
8.	Rolls clay into balls			

A	PERFECT DEMONSTRATION OF SKILL	B	PROGRESSING TOWARDS SKILL	C	NEEDS IMPROVEMENT

SKILLS AND COMPETENCIES

LISTENING AND SPEAKING SKILLS		A	B	C
1.	Recognises sounds and rhymes			
2.	Follows instructions			
3.	Asks and answers questions			
4.	Listen to stories			
5.	Speaks clearly			
6.	Repeats rhymes with actions			
7.	Tells stories using pictures			
8.	Describes experiences			

WRITING AND CREATIVE SKILLS		A	B	C
1.	Traces patterns, letters and objects			
2.	Fills colours			
3.	Writes letters and words			
4.	Writes missing letters			
5.	Draws and matches objects			
6.	Makes models by using clay & paper			
7.	Predicts what comes next			
8.	Solving easy puzzles & problems			

A	PERFECT DEMONSTRATION OF SKILL	B	PROGRESSING TOWARDS SKILL	C	NEEDS IMPROVEMENT

SKILLS AND COMPETENCIES

	LIFE SKILLS	A	B	C
1.	Hand and eye coordination			
2.	Eats on his or her own			
3.	Ask for help if needed			
4.	Sharing with others			
5.	Expresses likes and dislikes			
6.	Shows gratitude and thanks			
7.	Shows respect and kindness to elders			
8.	Cares for others, animals and plants			

	VISUAL & DISCRIMINATION SKILLS	A	B	C
1.	Identifies objects, pictures & persons			
2.	Finds the object or person in the pic			
3.	Sorts objects of same size & colour			
4.	Matches objects			
5.	Finds the odd one out			
6.	Understands the position & direction			
7.	Identifies the shapes, colours & size			
8.	Understand the distance			

Teacher's Signature	

A	PERFECT DEMONSTRATION OF SKILL	**B**	PROGRESSING TOWARDS SKILL	**C**	NEEDS IMPROVEMENT

PHYSICAL DEVELOPMENT

GROSS MOTOR SKILLS		A	B	C
1.	Walks with proper balance			
2.	Hops on one foot			
3.	Jumps			
4.	Catches and throws a ball			
5.	Steps over circles			
6.	Marches with swinging arms			
7.	Skips			
8.	Balances on one foot			

FINE MOTOR SKILLS		A	B	C
1.	Tears newspaper into strips			
2.	Crushes paper into ball			
3.	Picks up tiny objects			
4.	Buttons shirts			
5.	Draws in wet sand			
6.	Opens and closes the door			
7.	Builds tower with building blocks			
8.	Rolls clay into balls			

A PERFECT DEMONSTRATION OF SKILL   **B** PROGRESSING TOWARDS SKILL   **C** NEEDS IMPROVEMENT

SKILLS AND COMPETENCIES

	LISTENING AND SPEAKING SKILLS	A	B	C
1.	Recognises sounds and rhymes			
2.	Follows instructions			
3.	Asks and answers questions			
4.	Listen to stories			
5.	Speaks clearly			
6.	Repeats rhymes with actions			
7.	Tells stories using pictures			
8.	Describes experiences			

	WRITING AND CREATIVE SKILLS	A	B	C
1.	Traces patterns, letters and objects			
2.	Fills colours			
3.	Writes letters and words			
4.	Writes missing letters			
5.	Draws and matches objects			
6.	Makes models by using clay & paper			
7.	Predicts what comes next			
8.	Solving easy puzzles & problems			

A	PERFECT DEMONSTRATION OF SKILL	B	PROGRESSING TOWARDS SKILL	C	NEEDS IMPROVEMENT

SKILLS AND COMPETENCIES

LIFE SKILLS		A	B	C
1.	Hand and eye coordination			
2.	Eats on his or her own			
3.	Ask for help if needed			
4.	Sharing with others			
5.	Expresses likes and dislikes			
6.	Shows gratitude and thanks			
7.	Shows respect and kindness to elders			
8.	Cares for others, animals and plants			

VISUAL & DISCRIMINATION SKILLS		A	B	C
1.	Identifies objects, pictures & persons			
2.	Finds the object or person in the pic			
3.	Sorts objects of same size & colour			
4.	Matches objects			
5.	Finds the odd one out			
6.	Understands the position & direction			
7.	Identifies the shapes, colours & size			
8.	Understand the distance			

Teacher's Signature	

A	PERFECT DEMONSTRATION OF SKILL	B	PROGRESSING TOWARDS SKILL	C	NEEDS IMPROVEMENT

STUDENT'S DETAILS

1.	Name	
2.	Roll number	
3.	Class	
4.	Age	
5.	Section	

PHYSICAL DEVELOPMENT

GROSS MOTOR SKILLS		A	B	C
1.	Walks with proper balance			
2.	Hops on one foot			
3.	Jumps			
4.	Catches and throws a ball			
5.	Steps over circles			
6.	Marches with swinging arms			
7.	Skips			
8.	Balances on one foot			

FINE MOTOR SKILLS		A	B	C
1.	Tears newspaper into strips			
2.	Crushes paper into ball			
3.	Picks up tiny objects			
4.	Buttons shirts			
5.	Draws in wet sand			
6.	Opens and closes the door			
7.	Builds tower with building blocks			
8.	Rolls clay into balls			

A	PERFECT DEMONSTRATION OF SKILL	**B**	PROGRESSING TOWARDS SKILL	**C**	NEEDS IMPROVEMENT

NAME : _____

SKILLS AND COMPETENCIES

LISTENING AND SPEAKING SKILLS		A	B	C
1.	Recognises sounds and rhymes			
2.	Follows instructions			
3.	Asks and answers questions			
4.	Listen to stories			
5.	Speaks clearly			
6.	Repeats rhymes with actions			
7.	Tells stories using pictures			
8.	Describes experiences			

WRITING AND CREATIVE SKILLS		A	B	C
1.	Traces patterns, letters and objects			
2.	Fills colours			
3.	Writes letters and words			
4.	Writes missing letters			
5.	Draws and matches objects			
6.	Makes models by using clay & paper			
7.	Predicts what comes next			
8.	Solving easy puzzles & problems			

A PERFECT DEMONSTRATION OF SKILL	**B** PROGRESSING TOWARDS SKILL	**C** NEEDS IMPROVEMENT

SKILLS AND COMPETENCIES

	LIFE SKILLS	A	B	C
1.	Hand and eye coordination			
2.	Eats on his or her own			
3.	Ask for help if needed			
4.	Sharing with others			
5.	Expresses likes and dislikes			
6.	Shows gratitude and thanks			
7.	Shows respect and kindness to elders			
8.	Cares for others, animals and plants			

	VISUAL & DISCRIMINATION SKILLS	A	B	C
1.	Identifies objects, pictures & persons			
2.	Finds the object or person in the pic			
3.	Sorts objects of same size & colour			
4.	Matches objects			
5.	Finds the odd one out			
6.	Understands the position & direction			
7.	Identifies the shapes, colours & size			
8.	Understand the distance			

Teacher's Signature	

A	PERFECT DEMONSTRATION OF SKILL	B	PROGRESSING TOWARDS SKILL	C	NEEDS IMPROVEMENT

PHYSICAL DEVELOPMENT

GROSS MOTOR SKILLS		A	B	C
1.	Walks with proper balance			
2.	Hops on one foot			
3.	Jumps			
4.	Catches and throws a ball			
5.	Steps over circles			
6.	Marches with swinging arms			
7.	Skips			
8.	Balances on one foot			

FINE MOTOR SKILLS		A	B	C
1.	Tears newspaper into strips			
2.	Crushes paper into ball			
3.	Picks up tiny objects			
4.	Buttons shirts			
5.	Draws in wet sand			
6.	Opens and closes the door			
7.	Builds tower with building blocks			
8.	Rolls clay into balls			

A	PERFECT DEMONSTRATION OF SKILL	B	PROGRESSING TOWARDS SKILL	C	NEEDS IMPROVEMENT

SKILLS AND COMPETENCIES

LISTENING AND SPEAKING SKILLS	A	B	C
1. Recognises sounds and rhymes			
2. Follows instructions			
3. Asks and answers questions			
4. Listen to stories			
5. Speaks clearly			
6. Repeats rhymes with actions			
7. Tells stories using pictures			
8. Describes experiences			

WRITING AND CREATIVE SKILLS	A	B	C
1. Traces patterns, letters and objects			
2. Fills colours			
3. Writes letters and words			
4. Writes missing letters			
5. Draws and matches objects			
6. Makes models by using clay & paper			
7. Predicts what comes next			
8. Solving easy puzzles & problems			

A	PERFECT DEMONSTRATION OF SKILL	**B**	PROGRESSING TOWARDS SKILL	**C**	NEEDS IMPROVEMENT

SKILLS AND COMPETENCIES

	LIFE SKILLS	A	B	C
1.	Hand and eye coordination			
2.	Eats on his or her own			
3.	Ask for help if needed			
4.	Sharing with others			
5.	Expresses likes and dislikes			
6.	Shows gratitude and thanks			
7.	Shows respect and kindness to elders			
8.	Cares for others, animals and plants			

	VISUAL & DISCRIMINATION SKILLS	A	B	C
1.	Identifies objects, pictures & persons			
2.	Finds the object or person in the pic			
3.	Sorts objects of same size & colour			
4.	Matches objects			
5.	Finds the odd one out			
6.	Understands the position & direction			
7.	Identifies the shapes, colours & size			
8.	Understand the distance			

Teacher's Signature	

A	PERFECT DEMONSTRATION OF SKILL	B	PROGRESSING TOWARDS SKILL	C	NEEDS IMPROVEMENT

PHYSICAL DEVELOPMENT

	GROSS MOTOR SKILLS	A	B	C
1.	Walks with proper balance			
2.	Hops on one foot			
3.	Jumps			
4.	Catches and throws a ball			
5.	Steps over circles			
6.	Marches with swinging arms			
7.	Skips			
8.	Balances on one foot			

	FINE MOTOR SKILLS	A	B	C
1.	Tears newspaper into strips			
2.	Crushes paper into ball			
3.	Picks up tiny objects			
4.	Buttons shirts			
5.	Draws in wet sand			
6.	Opens and closes the door			
7.	Builds tower with building blocks			
8.	Rolls clay into balls			

A	PERFECT DEMONSTRATION OF SKILL	B	PROGRESSING TOWARDS SKILL	C	NEEDS IMPROVEMENT

ASSESSMENT - 3

NAME : _____

SKILLS AND COMPETENCIES

LISTENING AND SPEAKING SKILLS		A	B	C
1.	Recognises sounds and rhymes			
2.	Follows instructions			
3.	Asks and answers questions			
4.	Listen to stories			
5.	Speaks clearly			
6.	Repeats rhymes with actions			
7.	Tells stories using pictures			
8.	Describes experiences			

WRITING AND CREATIVE SKILLS		A	B	C
1.	Traces patterns, letters and objects			
2.	Fills colours			
3.	Writes letters and words			
4.	Writes missing letters			
5.	Draws and matches objects			
6.	Makes models by using clay & paper			
7.	Predicts what comes next			
8.	Solving easy puzzles & problems			

A	PERFECT DEMONSTRATION OF SKILL	B	PROGRESSING TOWARDS SKILL	C	NEEDS IMPROVEMENT

SKILLS AND COMPETENCIES

	LIFE SKILLS	A	B	C
1.	Hand and eye coordination			
2.	Eats on his or her own			
3.	Ask for help if needed			
4.	Sharing with others			
5.	Expresses likes and dislikes			
6.	Shows gratitude and thanks			
7.	Shows respect and kindness to elders			
8.	Cares for others, animals and plants			

	VISUAL & DISCRIMINATION SKILLS	A	B	C
1.	Identifies objects, pictures & persons			
2.	Finds the object or person in the pic			
3.	Sorts objects of same size & colour			
4.	Matches objects			
5.	Finds the odd one out			
6.	Understands the position & direction			
7.	Identifies the shapes, colours & size			
8.	Understand the distance			

Teacher's Signature	

A	PERFECT DEMONSTRATION OF SKILL	**B**	PROGRESSING TOWARDS SKILL	**C**	NEEDS IMPROVEMENT

STUDENT'S DETAILS

1.	Name	
2.	Roll number	
3.	Class	
4.	Age	
5.	Section	

PHYSICAL DEVELOPMENT

GROSS MOTOR SKILLS	A	B	C
1. Walks with proper balance			
2. Hops on one foot			
3. Jumps			
4. Catches and throws a ball			
5. Steps over circles			
6. Marches with swinging arms			
7. Skips			
8. Balances on one foot			

FINE MOTOR SKILLS	A	B	C
1. Tears newspaper into strips			
2. Crushes paper into ball			
3. Picks up tiny objects			
4. Buttons shirts			
5. Draws in wet sand			
6. Opens and closes the door			
7. Builds tower with building blocks			
8. Rolls clay into balls			

A	PERFECT DEMONSTRATION OF SKILL	B	PROGRESSING TOWARDS SKILL	C	NEEDS IMPROVEMENT

SKILLS AND COMPETENCIES

	LISTENING AND SPEAKING SKILLS	A	B	C
1.	Recognises sounds and rhymes			
2.	Follows instructions			
3.	Asks and answers questions			
4.	Listen to stories			
5.	Speaks clearly			
6.	Repeats rhymes with actions			
7.	Tells stories using pictures			
8.	Describes experiences			

	WRITING AND CREATIVE SKILLS	A	B	C
1.	Traces patterns, letters and objects			
2.	Fills colours			
3.	Writes letters and words			
4.	Writes missing letters			
5.	Draws and matches objects			
6.	Makes models by using clay & paper			
7.	Predicts what comes next			
8.	Solving easy puzzles & problems			

A	PERFECT DEMONSTRATION OF SKILL	B	PROGRESSING TOWARDS SKILL	C	NEEDS IMPROVEMENT

SKILLS AND COMPETENCIES

	LIFE SKILLS	A	B	C
1.	Hand and eye coordination			
2.	Eats on his or her own			
3.	Ask for help if needed			
4.	Sharing with others			
5.	Expresses likes and dislikes			
6.	Shows gratitude and thanks			
7.	Shows respect and kindness to elders			
8.	Cares for others, animals and plants			

	VISUAL & DISCRIMINATION SKILLS	A	B	C
1.	Identifies objects, pictures & persons			
2.	Finds the object or person in the pic			
3.	Sorts objects of same size & colour			
4.	Matches objects			
5.	Finds the odd one out			
6.	Understands the position & direction			
7.	Identifies the shapes, colours & size			
8.	Understand the distance			

Teacher's Signature	

A	PERFECT DEMONSTRATION OF SKILL	**B**	PROGRESSING TOWARDS SKILL	**C**	NEEDS IMPROVEMENT

PHYSICAL DEVELOPMENT

GROSS MOTOR SKILLS	A	B	C
1. Walks with proper balance			
2. Hops on one foot			
3. Jumps			
4. Catches and throws a ball			
5. Steps over circles			
6. Marches with swinging arms			
7. Skips			
8. Balances on one foot			

FINE MOTOR SKILLS	A	B	C
1. Tears newspaper into strips			
2. Crushes paper into ball			
3. Picks up tiny objects			
4. Buttons shirts			
5. Draws in wet sand			
6. Opens and closes the door			
7. Builds tower with building blocks			
8. Rolls clay into balls			

A PERFECT DEMONSTRATION OF SKILL	**B** PROGRESSING TOWARDS SKILL	**C** NEEDS IMPROVEMENT

SKILLS AND COMPETENCIES

	LISTENING AND SPEAKING SKILLS	A	B	C
1.	Recognises sounds and rhymes			
2.	Follows instructions			
3.	Asks and answers questions			
4.	Listen to stories			
5.	Speaks clearly			
6.	Repeats rhymes with actions			
7.	Tells stories using pictures			
8.	Describes experiences			

	WRITING AND CREATIVE SKILLS	A	B	C
1.	Traces patterns, letters and objects			
2.	Fills colours			
3.	Writes letters and words			
4.	Writes missing letters			
5.	Draws and matches objects			
6.	Makes models by using clay & paper			
7.	Predicts what comes next			
8.	Solving easy puzzles & problems			

A	PERFECT DEMONSTRATION OF SKILL	B	PROGRESSING TOWARDS SKILL	C	NEEDS IMPROVEMENT

SKILLS AND COMPETENCIES

	LIFE SKILLS	A	B	C
1.	Hand and eye coordination			
2.	Eats on his or her own			
3.	Ask for help if needed			
4.	Sharing with others			
5.	Expresses likes and dislikes			
6.	Shows gratitude and thanks			
7.	Shows respect and kindness to elders			
8.	Cares for others, animals and plants			

	VISUAL & DISCRIMINATION SKILLS	A	B	C
1.	Identifies objects, pictures & persons			
2.	Finds the object or person in the pic			
3.	Sorts objects of same size & colour			
4.	Matches objects			
5.	Finds the odd one out			
6.	Understands the position & direction			
7.	Identifies the shapes, colours & size			
8.	Understand the distance			

Teacher's Signature	

A	PERFECT DEMONSTRATION OF SKILL	B	PROGRESSING TOWARDS SKILL	C	NEEDS IMPROVEMENT

PHYSICAL DEVELOPMENT

GROSS MOTOR SKILLS	A	B	C
1.	Walks with proper balance			
2.	Hops on one foot			
3.	Jumps			
4.	Catches and throws a ball			
5.	Steps over circles			
6.	Marches with swinging arms			
7.	Skips			
8.	Balances on one foot			

FINE MOTOR SKILLS	A	B	C
1.	Tears newspaper into strips			
2.	Crushes paper into ball			
3.	Picks up tiny objects			
4.	Buttons shirts			
5.	Draws in wet sand			
6.	Opens and closes the door			
7.	Builds tower with building blocks			
8.	Rolls clay into balls			

| A | PERFECT DEMONSTRATION OF SKILL | B | PROGRESSING TOWARDS SKILL | C | NEEDS IMPROVEMENT |

SKILLS AND COMPETENCIES

LISTENING AND SPEAKING SKILLS	A	B	C
1. Recognises sounds and rhymes			
2. Follows instructions			
3. Asks and answers questions			
4. Listen to stories			
5. Speaks clearly			
6. Repeats rhymes with actions			
7. Tells stories using pictures			
8. Describes experiences			

WRITING AND CREATIVE SKILLS	A	B	C
1. Traces patterns, letters and objects			
2. Fills colours			
3. Writes letters and words			
4. Writes missing letters			
5. Draws and matches objects			
6. Makes models by using clay & paper			
7. Predicts what comes next			
8. Solving easy puzzles & problems			

A PERFECT DEMONSTRATION OF SKILL	**B** PROGRESSING TOWARDS SKILL	**C** NEEDS IMPROVEMENT

SKILLS AND COMPETENCIES

	LIFE SKILLS	A	B	C
1.	Hand and eye coordination			
2.	Eats on his or her own			
3.	Ask for help if needed			
4.	Sharing with others			
5.	Expresses likes and dislikes			
6.	Shows gratitude and thanks			
7.	Shows respect and kindness to elders			
8.	Cares for others, animals and plants			

	VISUAL & DISCRIMINATION SKILLS	A	B	C
1.	Identifies objects, pictures & persons			
2.	Finds the object or person in the pic			
3.	Sorts objects of same size & colour			
4.	Matches objects			
5.	Finds the odd one out			
6.	Understands the position & direction			
7.	Identifies the shapes, colours & size			
8.	Understand the distance			

Teacher's Signature	

A	PERFECT DEMONSTRATION OF SKILL	**B**	PROGRESSING TOWARDS SKILL	**C**	NEEDS IMPROVEMENT

Made in United States
Troutdale, OR
07/26/2023

11565152R10080